Geo-Politics Made Simple

Table of Contents

The Role of Natural Resources in Shaping Global Power Dynamics

Cyber Geopolitics and National Security

Climate Change and Geopolitical Stability

Economic Sanctions and Geopolitical Strategies

The Belt and Road Initiative: Implications for Global Geopolitics

The exploration of Space and Geopolitics: The Final Frontier

The exploration of "Energy Geopolitics: Shifting Power Dynamics in the Global Energy Landscape"

Water Scarcity and Geopolitical Tensions

Arctic Geopolitics: Balancing Environmental Preservation and Resource Exploitation

Maritime Security in the South China Sea: Geopolitical Tensions and Regional Stability

Cyber-security and Geopolitics: Navigating the Digital Frontier

Climate Change and Geopolitics: Navigating Environmental Challenges

Geopolitical Implications of Artificial Intelligence: Shaping the Future Landscape

Renewable Energy and Geopolitics: Shifting Power Dynamics in the Energy Landscape

Space Exploration and Geopolitics: The New Frontier

Blockchain Technology and Geopolitics: Transforming Trust and Security

Biotechnology and Geopolitics: Redefining Health and Security

Renewable Energy and Geopolitics: Shifting Power Dynamics in the Energy Landscape

Cyber-security and Geopolitics: Securing the Digital Frontier

Artificial Intelligence and Geopolitics: Shaping the Future Landscape

Exporting Values: The Geopolitical Implications of Promoting Democracy and Human Rights

Dollars and Dominance: The Role of Currency in Geopolitical Strategy

Soft Power Strategies: The Role of Cultural Diplomacy in Shaping Geopolitical Landscapes

Brexit and Beyond: Implications for European Stability and Geopolitical Alliances

United Nations or Divided States? The Geopolitical Role of International Organizations

Shifting Sands: The Complex Geopolitical Dynamics of the Middle East

A Continent in Transition: Africa's Emerging Geopolitical Landscape

In the Shadow of Giants: Latin America's Geopolitical Position between the US and China

Cold Front: The Rising Geopolitical Importance of the Arctic Region

Storytelling States: The Role of Geopolitical Narratives in Shaping National Identity

The Role of Natural Resources in Shaping Global Power Dynamics

Exploring the geopolitical implications of Arctic oil reserves requires delving into a multifaceted domain where environmental concerns, sovereignty disputes, and the shifting sands of international power dynamics intersect. The Arctic, with its vast and largely untapped resources, emerges as a critical arena for understanding the interplay between natural wealth and geopolitical strategy. This intricate dance involves various actors, each with their strategic interests, set against the backdrop of an environment that is both fragile and harsh.

At the heart of the Arctic geopolitical saga are the sovereignty and territorial claims made by the Arctic states: Canada, Denmark (through Greenland), Norway, Russia, and the United States. Each of these nations asserts rights over portions of the Arctic, driven by the desire to access its valuable oil reserves. The disputes arise from overlapping claims, where the boundaries of one nation's claimed territory intersect with another's. These claims are not merely academic; they have real implications for the control of resources, navigation rights, and military strategy in the region.

For instance, Russia and Canada have submitted competing claims to the United Nations to extend their territories over the same swath of the Arctic seabed, believed to be rich in oil and gas. The resolution of these disputes hinges on international law, specifically the United Nations Convention on the Law of the Sea (UNCLOS), which provides a framework for defining the limits of a country's exclusive economic zone (up to 200 nautical miles from their coastline) and their continental shelf. The complexity arises when countries argue that their continental shelf extends beyond this limit, based on geological and hydro-graphic data. These disputes are not only about economic gains but also about national pride and strategic military positioning.

The quest for Arctic oil is fraught with environmental hazards. The Arctic ecosystem is particularly vulnerable to disturbances due to its cold climate and the presence of ice-covered waters for much of the year. Oil exploration and extraction pose significant risks, including oil spills, which could have devastating effects on marine life and the broader ecosystem. Moreover, the exploitation of Arctic oil resources stands in stark contradiction to global efforts to combat climate change by reducing reliance on fossil fuels.

The Arctic's unique biodiversity, including species such as polar bears, walruses, and various seabirds, is at risk from oil drilling operations. An oil spill in the Arctic's remote and icy waters would be significantly more challenging to clean up than in other regions, owing to the lack of infrastructure, the difficulties presented by ice cover, and the area's isolation. The 1989 Exxon Valdez oil spill off Alaska, while not in the high Arctic, provides a cautionary tale of the long-lasting impact of oil spills in cold environments. The continued push for Arctic oil extraction highlights the tension between economic development and environmental stewardship, necessitating rigorous environmental safeguards and emergency response strategies.

The Arctic oil reserves are not just economic assets; they're strategic levers in the global power game. For Arctic states, these resources offer a means to bolster national economies and assert greater influence on the international stage. For non-Arctic states, such as China, the Arctic represents new opportunities for energy security and strategic investments, marking the extension of their geopolitical interests into this polar region.

China's Arctic strategy, often referred to as the "Polar Silk Road," underscores this point. By investing in Arctic research, infrastructure projects, and resource exploration, China aims to secure a stake in the region's future, ensuring access to its resources and potentially lucrative shipping routes as Arctic ice melts. This strategy has prompted Arctic nations to reassess their own policies and alliances, wary of China's growing influence. The involvement of global powers in the Arctic also underscores the potential for the region to become a new frontier in geopolitical rivalry, requiring careful diplomacy to manage competing interests and maintain peace and stability.

The Arctic's oil reserves sit at a nexus of competing interests, embodying the challenges of balancing economic development, environmental integrity, and geopolitical stability. As nations navigate these waters, the decisions made today will shape the Arctic's future and, by extension, the global order. Effective governance, international cooperation, and a commitment to sustainable development principles are essential to harnessing the Arctic's potential in a manner that respects its environmental limits and the rights of Indigenous peoples. The story of Arctic oil is not just about the quest for energy; it's a chapter in the on-going narrative of how humanity interacts with our planet's most remote and fragile regions.

Cyber Geopolitics and National Security

The exploration of "Cyber Geopolitics and National Security" delves into a domain where the digital landscape intersects with global power dynamics, highlighting the crucial role of cyber-security in the preservation of national security and the unfolding of international relations. This intricate web of interactions reveals how digital infrastructure becomes a battleground for state actors, non-state entities, and individuals, influencing everything from electoral processes to the global economy.

The cyber domain represents the fifth dimension of warfare, alongside land, sea, air, and space. It encompasses a virtual battleground where state and non-state actors engage in espionage, sabotage, and influence operations. This realm is defined by its lack of physical borders, allowing for actions that can be conducted remotely, often anonymously, with significant impacts on real-world security and diplomatic relations.

For instance, cyber espionage activities, such as the theft of sensitive government data or industrial secrets, can shift the balance of power between nations without firing a single bullet.

Similarly, sabotage operations, like the Stuxnet virus attack on Iranian nuclear facilities, demonstrate how cyber tools can be used to achieve strategic objectives traditionally pursued through kinetic military actions. These incidents underscore the cyber domain's potential to disrupt national security apparatus and international peace without direct confrontation.

In the face of these challenges, cyber-security emerges as a fundamental pillar of national security. Governments worldwide are investing heavily in defensive and offensive cyber capabilities, recognizing that protecting digital infrastructure is as crucial as safeguarding physical borders. This shift marks the recognition that national security in the 21st century encompasses not only military and economic power but also digital resilience and sovereignty.

The establishment of dedicated cyber-security agencies, such as the United States Cyber Command (USCYBERCOM) or the UK's National Cyber Security Centre (NCSC), illustrates this trend. These organizations are tasked with protecting critical infrastructure, such as power grids and financial systems, from cyber-attacks that could have devastating effects on national economies and public safety. Moreover, these entities develop offensive capabilities, signalling a readiness to engage in cyber warfare as a means of national defence and as a deterrent against potential aggressors.

Cyber operations extend beyond espionage and sabotage; they also encompass influence operations aimed at shaping public opinion, interfering in electoral processes, and undermining trust in institutions. The cyber domain offers a powerful platform for disseminating propaganda, disinformation, and fake news, with profound implications for democracy, governance, and international diplomacy.

The alleged interference in the 2016 United States presidential election and other electoral processes worldwide highlights the cyber domain's role in shaping political outcomes. Through social media platforms and other digital channels, state and non-state actors can launch sophisticated disinformation campaigns to polarize societies, sow discord, and manipulate public opinion. These tactics, often cheaper and more effective than traditional military interventions, represent a form of soft power in the cyber age, where controlling information flows can translate into geopolitical leverage.

As nations navigate this new frontier, the interplay between cyber-security measures, offensive cyber operations, and information warfare will increasingly define international relations and national security strategies. The challenges and opportunities presented by the cyber domain require a nuanced understanding of technology, law, and ethics, as well as robust international cooperation to establish norms and prevent escalations. In this ever-evolving landscape, the ability to protect and project national interests through digital means will be a determinant of state power, necessitating on-going adaptation and innovation in cyber-security policies and practices.

Climate Change and Geopolitical Stability

"Climate Change and Geopolitical Stability2, explores the intricate relationships between the evolving climate crisis and its profound effects on international peace and security. This investigation sheds light on how climate-induced changes—such as rising sea levels, extreme weather events, and resource scarcity—serve as catalysts for geopolitical tension and conflict, while also offering opportunities for unprecedented global cooperation.

Climate change is increasingly recognized as a 'threat multiplier,' exacerbating existing vulnerabilities within and between nations. It does not respect national borders, and its impacts are felt most acutely on the global stage, influencing migration patterns, access to resources, and the strategic military landscape.

For instance, the shrinking ice in the Arctic opens new maritime routes and access to untapped natural resources, leading to sovereignty disputes among Arctic nations. Meanwhile, in regions like Sub-Saharan Africa and the Middle East, prolonged droughts and water scarcity heighten competition for precious resources, increasing the risk of internal conflicts and cross-border tensions. These scenarios highlight how climate change acts as a catalyst, intensifying existing geopolitical fissures and creating new areas of contention.

One of the most direct ways in which climate change impacts geopolitical stability is through the scarcity of essential resources, such as water, food, and arable land. As climate conditions change, regions that once provided ample resources can become barren, leading to competition and, in some cases, conflict.

The conflict in Darfur, often cited as the first major climate change conflict, illustrates how diminishing resources can exacerbate existing social tensions. Here, prolonged drought and desertification led to competition between farmers and herders over dwindling water supplies and fertile land, igniting a conflict that claimed hundreds of thousands of lives. Such instances underscore the potential for climate-induced resource scarcity to spark violence and destabilize regions.

Climate change is a significant driver of forced migration and displacement, as people move in response to extreme weather events, sea-level rise, and deteriorating environmental conditions. This mass movement of people poses challenges to national security, social cohesion, and international diplomacy.

The Syrian civil war, preceded by the country's worst drought on record, serves as a poignant example of how climate-induced displacement can contribute to geopolitical instability. The drought led to widespread crop failure and the mass migration of rural populations into urban centres, exacerbating socio-economic pressures and contributing to the unrest that spiralled into conflict. As climate change continues to impact global weather patterns, such displacement is expected to increase, presenting significant challenges for receiving communities and international relations.

While climate change presents considerable challenges to geopolitical stability, it also offers a unique opportunity for international cooperation. The global nature of the climate crisis requires concerted action from all nations, transcending traditional geopolitical rivalries and fostering collaboration.

The Paris Agreement on climate change is a prime example of how nations can come together to address a common threat. By committing to limit global warming and enhance climate resilience, countries acknowledge the interconnectedness of their fates and the necessity of joint action. Such international agreements lay the groundwork for cooperative approaches to shared challenges, promoting peace and stability through collective effort.

From resource scarcity and forced migration to opportunities for international cooperation, the impacts of climate change are profoundly reshaping the geopolitical landscape. Navigating this new terrain requires a nuanced understanding of environmental dynamics and a commitment to collaborative, sustainable solutions. As the world grapples with the escalating climate crisis, the ability to adapt to and mitigate these changes will be paramount in maintaining global stability and fostering a peaceful international order.

Economic Sanctions and Geopolitical Strategies

The exploration of "Economic Sanctions and Geopolitical Strategies" delves into the complex interplay between the imposition of economic sanctions and their ramifications on global geopolitical dynamics. This discourse unpacks the strategic use of sanctions by nations as tools for achieving foreign policy objectives, underscoring the implications for international relations, economic stability, and the sovereignty of targeted nations.

Economic sanctions are deployed by countries or international bodies to coerce, deter, or punish nations that violate international norms, engage in aggressive actions, or threaten global peace. These sanctions can take various forms, including trade barriers, tariffs, restrictions on financial transactions, and the freezing of assets. While ostensibly aimed at enforcing international law and promoting global security, the strategic use of sanctions often reflects the geopolitical interests of the imposing countries.

The United States' sanctions on Iran over its nuclear program illustrate how sanctions serve as tools of foreign policy. These sanctions, which include restrictions on oil exports and access to the international banking system, aim to pressure Iran into complying with international nuclear agreements. However, they also reflect broader U.S. strategic interests in the Middle East, including deterring regional aggression and curtailing Iran's influence. This example highlights how sanctions are a preferred instrument in the geopolitical toolkit, used to navigate the complex web of international relations without resorting to military conflict.

Sanctions influence international relations not just between the imposing country and the target, but also among global actors more broadly. They can lead to shifts in alliances, affect global markets, and provoke responses that range from compliance to retaliation.

Russia's annexation of Crimea in 2014 and the subsequent sanctions imposed by Western countries demonstrate the ripple effects of sanctions on international relations. The sanctions, targeting key sectors of the Russian economy and individuals close to the government, aimed to isolate Russia internationally. In response, Russia sought to deepen ties with non-Western powers, such as China, and looked for alternative markets and financial systems to circumvent the sanctions. This situation underscores how sanctions can alter the landscape of international alliances and economic relationships, prompting both targeted and imposing states to seek new partnerships.

While intended to pressure governments, economic sanctions often have profound effects on the civilian population of targeted countries, leading to economic hardship, shortages of essential goods, and deterioration of living conditions. The humanitarian impact of sanctions raises ethical questions about their use and effectiveness.

The comprehensive sanctions imposed on Iraq in the 1990s, intended to compel Saddam Hussein's compliance with disarmament obligations, resulted in widespread humanitarian crises, including severe malnutrition and a collapse of the healthcare system. Critics argue that such outcomes highlight the moral dilemma of sanctions that, while aimed at punishing regimes, disproportionately affect innocent civilians. This example illustrates the need for carefully calibrated sanctions that target regimes and their supporters directly, minimizing the collateral damage to the broader population.

Sanctions are a double-edged sword; they can isolate and weaken targeted nations, but they also have potential repercussions for the imposing countries and the global economy. The interconnected nature of the modern global economy means sanctions can have unintended consequences, affecting the economic interests of imposing states and causing disruptions in global markets.

The sanctions on Russia have impacted European countries by reducing the flow of Russian natural gas, leading to energy shortages and increased prices. This example highlights the interconnectedness of the global economy, where actions taken against one country can have unintended consequences for others, underscoring the complexity of employing economic sanctions as a geopolitical strategy.

While serving as critical tools for enforcing international norms and achieving foreign policy goals, sanctions also pose significant challenges, affecting international relations, economies, and civilian populations. As the global landscape evolves, the strategic deployment of sanctions requires a careful balance between achieving political objectives and mitigating unintended consequences, demanding a nuanced understanding of global dynamics and a commitment to diplomatic solutions.

The Belt and Road Initiative:

Implications for Global Geopolitics

The exploration of "The Belt and Road Initiative: Implications for Global Geopolitics" delves into China's ambitious infrastructure and economic development project spanning across Asia, Africa, and Europe. This analysis underscores the strategic dimensions of the Belt and Road Initiative (BRI) and its profound implications for international relations, global trade networks, and the balance of power in the 21st century.

Launched in 2013 by President Xi Jinping, the BRI aims to enhance global trade and stimulate economic growth across Asia and beyond through the development of trade routes reminiscent of the ancient Silk Road. It encompasses a vast network of railways, highways, maritime routes, and infrastructure projects designed to facilitate trade and investment, linking China to over 60 countries.

A hallmark project under the BRI is the China-Pakistan Economic Corridor (CPEC), which includes the development of highways, railways, and pipelines between Pakistan and China. It aims to provide China with direct access to the Arabian Sea, reducing reliance on the Strait of Malacca and enhancing its strategic presence in the Indian Ocean. This example illustrates the BRI's dual economic and strategic dimensions, where infrastructure projects serve both developmental goals and geopolitical ambitions.

The BRI has significant implications for global trade and investment patterns, potentially altering economic landscapes and creating new economic centres. By improving connectivity and reducing transportation costs, it promises to enhance the efficiency of international trade, but it also raises concerns about debt sustainability and economic sovereignty in participating countries.

In Sri Lanka, the Hambantota Port project financed through Chinese loans is often cited as an example of the "debt-trap diplomacy" associated with the BRI. When Sri Lanka struggled to repay the loans, it granted China a 99-year lease on the port, raising concerns about China's growing strategic foothold in the Indian Ocean. This scenario highlights the potential economic and geopolitical risks faced by countries participating in the BRI, questioning the balance between the benefits of infrastructure development and the implications for national sovereignty and economic independence.

The BRI represents a strategic effort by China to reshape global power dynamics, positioning itself as a leading force in global affairs. By extending its influence across critical regions, China aims to challenge the traditional power structures and establish a new order that reflects its interests and values.

The BRI's expansion into Central Asia and Eastern Europe is indicative of China's intent to carve out a sphere of influence in regions historically under Russian and Western influence, respectively. This strategic manoeuvring prompts a realignment of regional powers and necessitates adjustments in the foreign policies of affected nations. The initiative thereby acts as a catalyst for a new geopolitical landscape, where China's growing economic footprint translates into increased political and strategic leverage.

The BRI has elicited varied responses from other global powers, particularly the United States and the European Union, who view China's initiative with a mix of scepticism and strategic caution. Concerns revolve around the transparency, governance, and strategic intentions behind the BRI, leading to calls for alternative development models that emphasize sustainability, fairness, and respect for international norms.

The establishment of the Blue Dot Network by the United States, Japan, and Australia serves as a counter-initiative to the BRI, offering a certification scheme for infrastructure projects based on quality and sustainability standards. This initiative reflects an attempt to provide countries with alternatives to Chinese investments, emphasizing the importance of maintaining a rules-based international order and countering China's influence by promoting high-standard global infrastructure development.

While offering significant opportunities for economic development and global connectivity, the BRI also raises critical questions about debt dependency, sovereignty, and the shifting balance of global power. As the BRI continues to unfold, its long-term success and geopolitical implications will largely depend on China's ability to navigate the complex interplay of economic ambitions, strategic interests, and international responses, shaping the contours of the 21st-century global order.

The exploration of Space and Geopolitics:

The Final Frontier

The exploration of "Space and Geopolitics: The Final Frontier" delves into the increasingly significant role of space exploration, satellite technology, and space-based assets in shaping global geopolitics. This analysis underscores how advancements in space capabilities have profound implications for national security, economic competitiveness, and strategic influence among space-faring nations.

Space exploration has transitioned from a scientific endeavour to a strategic domain with immense geopolitical implications. Satellites play critical roles in communication, navigation, weather forecasting, and surveillance, making them indispensable assets for military, commercial, and civilian applications.

The Global Positioning System (GPS), operated by the United States, exemplifies the strategic significance of space assets. It provides precise positioning and timing information used in military operations, transportation, agriculture, finance, and countless other sectors, underpinning global connectivity and economic activity. The reliance of nations worldwide on GPS underscores its strategic value and the geopolitical leverage it affords the United States.

Space has become a contested domain, with nations investing in military space capabilities to protect their interests and project power. Space-based surveillance, reconnaissance, and communication systems play crucial roles in modern warfare, enabling situational awareness, command and control, and precision strikes.

China's anti-satellite (ASAT) missile test in 2007 highlighted the vulnerability of space assets and sparked concerns about the militarization of space. Similarly, the United States Space Force, established in 2019, reflects a growing recognition of space as a distinct war-fighting domain, with dedicated military organizations responsible for protecting and defending American space assets. These developments underscore the strategic importance of space capabilities in deterring adversaries and maintaining military superiority.

Space exploration also presents lucrative economic opportunities, attracting investments from governments, corporations, and entrepreneurs. The commercialization of space, including satellite launches, space tourism, asteroid mining, and satellite internet constellations, has the potential to reshape global industries and generate substantial economic returns.

SpaceX, founded by Elon Musk, exemplifies the commercialization of space exploration. The company's successful development of reusable rockets has dramatically reduced the cost of space access, opening up opportunities for satellite deployment, cargo resupply missions to the International Space Station (ISS), and future crewed missions to Mars. SpaceX's competitive pricing and innovative technologies have disrupted the traditional aerospace industry, prompting other players to adapt and innovate to remain competitive in the evolving space economy.

While space exploration offers opportunities for collaboration and peaceful cooperation, it also engenders competition and geopolitical rivalries among space-faring nations. The establishment of international treaties and agreements, such as the Outer Space Treaty and the Artemis Accords, seeks to regulate space activities and prevent conflict in the space domain.

The Artemis program, led by NASA with international partners, aims to return humans to the Moon and establish a sustainable lunar presence by the 2030s. While framed as a collaborative effort, the program also reflects geopolitical competition, with China and Russia developing their lunar exploration programs and ambitions. This competition mirrors the space race of the Cold War era, underscoring the strategic importance of space exploration in asserting national prestige and influence.

As nations invest in space capabilities for military, economic, and scientific purposes, the stakes in the space domain continue to rise. Balancing opportunities for cooperation with challenges of competition and conflict will be crucial in navigating the complexities of space geopolitics and harnessing the benefits of space exploration for the betterment of humanity. As we venture further into the cosmos, understanding and managing the geopolitics of

space will be paramount in ensuring a peaceful
and prosperous future for all.

The exploration of Energy Geopolitics:

Shifting Power Dynamics in

The Global Energy Landscape

The exploration of "Energy Geopolitics: Shifting Power Dynamics in the Global Energy Landscape" delves into the intricate interplay between energy resources, international relations, and strategic interests of nations. This analysis underscores how shifts in energy production, distribution, and consumption reshape geopolitical dynamics, influence foreign policies, and impact global stability.

The global energy landscape has undergone significant transformations over the past century, driven by advancements in technology, changes in energy demand, and shifts in geopolitical power. Traditional energy sources such as coal and oil have been supplemented by renewables like solar and wind, altering the geopolitical calculus of energy-producing and energy-dependent nations.

The rise of unconventional oil and gas extraction techniques, such as hydraulic fracturing (fracking) and shale oil production, has reshaped the global energy map. The United States, once heavily dependent on imported oil, has become a major oil and gas producer, reducing its reliance on energy imports and altering the dynamics of global energy markets. This shift has significant geopolitical implications, affecting traditional energy exporters like Russia and the Middle East and challenging their dominance in global energy trade.

Energy security, defined as the uninterrupted availability of energy resources at affordable prices, is a critical concern for nations worldwide. Dependence on foreign energy sources exposes countries to geopolitical risks, including supply disruptions, price volatility, and political manipulation by energy-exporting nations.

The European Union's efforts to diversify its energy sources illustrate the importance of energy security in geopolitical strategy. Projects like the Southern Gas Corridor, which aims to transport natural gas from the Caspian Sea region to Europe via pipelines, seek to reduce Europe's reliance on Russian gas imports and enhance its energy security. Similarly, China's Belt and Road Initiative includes energy infrastructure projects aimed at securing access to oil and gas resources and diversifying its energy supplies to meet growing demand.

The quest for energy resources often leads to competition and conflict over access to, and control of, valuable energy reserves. Territorial disputes in regions rich in oil and gas, such as the South China Sea and the Arctic, underscore how energy geopolitics intertwine with broader geopolitical rivalries and security concerns.

The South China Sea, a strategic waterway through which a significant portion of global trade passes, is also believed to contain vast oil and gas reserves. Competing territorial claims among countries bordering the South China Sea, notably China, Vietnam, the Philippines, and Malaysia, have led to heightened tensions and increased military presence in the region. These disputes highlight the intersection of energy interests, maritime security, and geopolitical rivalries, with the potential for escalation and conflict.

The rise of renewable energy sources presents new geopolitical opportunities and challenges. As countries transition towards cleaner energy sources to mitigate climate change, they also seek to capitalize on the economic and strategic benefits of renewable energy production and technology development.

Germany's Energiewende, or energy transition, exemplifies the geopolitical implications of renewable energy policies. By investing heavily in wind and solar power, Germany aims to reduce its dependence on fossil fuel imports, increase energy independence, and position itself as a global leader in clean energy technology. This transition not only contributes to Germany's energy security but also enhances its soft power and influence in international climate negotiations and renewable energy markets.

As nations navigate the complexities of the energy transition, they must balance strategic imperatives with environmental sustainability, economic development, and geopolitical stability. Understanding the interplay between energy production, distribution, and consumption is essential for addressing the geopolitical challenges of the 21st century and building a more resilient and sustainable global energy system.

Water Scarcity and Geopolitical Tensions

The examination of "Water Scarcity and Geopolitical Tensions" delves into the critical issue of water scarcity and its implications for global geopolitics. This analysis highlights how competition over scarce water resources, exacerbated by population growth, climate change, and unsustainable water management practices, can lead to heightened tensions, conflicts, and geopolitical instability.

Water scarcity has emerged as a pressing global challenge, affecting regions across the world and exacerbating socio-economic disparities. Population growth, urbanization, and industrialization place increasing pressure on finite water resources, leading to over-extraction, pollution, and depletion of freshwater sources.

The depletion of the Aral Sea in Central Asia serves as a poignant example of the consequences of water mismanagement. Once the world's fourth-largest lake, the Aral Sea has shrunk to a fraction of its former size due to diversion of its tributary rivers for irrigation purposes. This ecological disaster has devastated local ecosystems, disrupted livelihoods, and contributed to social unrest in the region, underscoring the far-reaching impacts of water scarcity on human security and geopolitical stability.

Competition over water resources has the potential to escalate into conflicts, both within and between nations, particularly in regions where water is scarce or unevenly distributed. Disputes over trans-0boundary rivers, shared aquifers, and access to water for irrigation, drinking, and industrial purposes can fuel tensions and exacerbate existing geopolitical rivalries.

The longstanding dispute between Egypt, Sudan, and Ethiopia over the Grand Ethiopian Renaissance Dam (GERD) on the Nile River epitomizes the geopolitical complexities of water management. Ethiopia's construction of the dam, which has the potential to significantly alter the flow of the Nile downstream, has raised concerns in downstream countries about water security and agricultural livelihoods. Diplomatic negotiations over the equitable distribution of Nile waters have been contentious, reflecting the geopolitical stakes involved in managing shared water resources.

Water scarcity also presents opportunities for cooperation and conflict resolution through water diplomacy and multilateral agreements. Collaborative approaches to water management, such as joint infrastructure projects, data sharing mechanisms, and dispute resolution mechanisms, can mitigate tensions and promote peace-building efforts.

The Mekong River Commission (MRC), established by riparian countries in Southeast Asia, exemplifies the potential of water diplomacy in managing shared river basins. Through the MRC, Cambodia, Laos, Thailand, and Vietnam cooperate on sustainable water management practices, data sharing, and impact assessments of proposed development projects. Despite geopolitical tensions among member states, the MRC serves as a forum for dialogue and cooperation, fostering mutual understanding and trust in addressing trans-boundary water challenges.

Climate change exacerbates water insecurity by altering precipitation patterns, increasing the frequency and intensity of extreme weather events, and accelerating glacial melt. These changes further strain water resources, heightening vulnerabilities and exacerbating socio-economic inequalities.

The Himalayan region, often referred to as the "water tower of Asia," faces escalating risks of water insecurity due to climate change-induced glacier melt. The loss of glaciers threatens the livelihoods of millions of people who depend on glacial melt-water for drinking, irrigation, and hydropower generation. As Himalayan glaciers recede, downstream countries like India, Bangladesh, and China face increased water stress, heightening the potential for conflict over shared river basins.

As water becomes an increasingly scarce and contested resource, nations must prioritize dialogue, diplomacy, and collective action to ensure equitable access, enhance resilience, and prevent conflicts over water resources. By addressing the root causes of water scarcity and promoting inclusive governance frameworks, the international community can mitigate

geopolitical tensions and build a more
sustainable and peaceful future for all.

Arctic Geopolitics:

Balancing Environmental Preservation and Resource Exploitation

The exploration of "Arctic Geopolitics: Balancing Environmental Preservation and Resource Exploitation" delves into the complex interplay between environmental conservation, resource extraction, and geopolitical interests in the Arctic region. This analysis highlights the challenges and opportunities posed by the melting ice caps and the opening of new maritime routes, presenting a delicate balance between economic development and environmental stewardship.

The melting of Arctic ice due to climate change has transformed the region into a new geopolitical arena, attracting attention from Arctic and non-Arctic states alike. The receding ice caps open up new opportunities for resource extraction, shipping routes, and strategic military positioning, while also raising concerns about environmental degradation and indigenous rights.

The Northwest Passage, once impassable due to ice cover, is now increasingly navigable during the summer months, offering a shortcut between the Atlantic and Pacific Oceans. This newfound accessibility has sparked interest from countries like China, which sees the Arctic as a potential maritime trade route and strategic corridor for its Belt and Road Initiative. The opening of the Arctic presents geopolitical opportunities and challenges, prompting debates over sovereignty, environmental protection, and economic development.

The Arctic region is rich in natural resources, including oil, gas, minerals, and fisheries, making it a tantalizing frontier for resource exploitation. Arctic states and energy companies are eyeing these reserves for economic development, energy security, and geopolitical influence, raising questions about the environmental impacts and sustainability of extractive industries.

Russia's Arctic energy strategy exemplifies the push for resource exploitation in the region. The Russian government has invested in offshore oil and gas exploration projects in the Arctic, such as the Yamal LNG project, to tap into the region's vast hydrocarbon reserves. These projects promise economic benefits for Russia but also raise concerns about the environmental risks of oil spills, habitat destruction, and greenhouse gas emissions. The pursuit of Arctic resources underscores the tensions between economic interests and environmental preservation in the region.

Indigenous communities in the Arctic, such as the Inuit, Saami, and Aleut peoples, have inhabited the region for millennia and rely on its pristine environment for their livelihoods and cultural heritage. The encroachment of resource extraction activities and the impacts of climate change threaten the traditional way of life and indigenous rights, highlighting the need for inclusive and sustainable development policies.

The Inuit of Canada's Nunavut territory are actively engaged in Arctic governance and environmental conservation efforts, advocating for indigenous rights and sustainable resource management practices. Organizations like the Inuit Circumpolar Council work to amplify indigenous voices in international forums, raising awareness of the impacts of climate change and advocating for policies that prioritize environmental protection and indigenous self-determination. Indigenous-led conservation initiatives serve as models for balancing economic development with cultural preservation and environmental stewardship in the Arctic.

The Arctic Council, an intergovernmental forum comprised of Arctic states and indigenous organizations, plays a central role in facilitating cooperation and governance in the region. Through the Arctic Council, member states collaborate on environmental protection, scientific research, search and rescue operations, and sustainable development, fostering dialogue and diplomatic relations in the Arctic.

The Arctic Council's agreement on the prevention of unregulated fishing in the central Arctic Ocean exemplifies the forum's role in addressing shared challenges through multilateral cooperation. By establishing binding measures to manage fish stocks in the high seas of the central Arctic Ocean, the agreement promotes sustainable fisheries management and ecosystem conservation in the region. Such collaborative initiatives demonstrate the potential for international cooperation to address the complex geopolitical, environmental, and socio-economic dynamics of the Arctic.

As the Arctic undergoes rapid transformations due to climate change and geopolitical shifts, it is imperative to prioritize sustainable development practices that respect the fragile Arctic ecosystem and the rights of indigenous communities. By fostering international cooperation, indigenous participation, and evidence-based policymaking, the Arctic can be managed as a shared resource, ensuring its preservation for future generations while responsibly harnessing its economic potential.

Maritime Security in the South China Sea:

Geopolitical Tensions and Regional Stability

The examination of "Maritime Security in the South China Sea: Geopolitical Tensions and Regional Stability" delves into the complex dynamics surrounding one of the most contentious maritime disputes in the world. This analysis sheds light on the geopolitical tensions arising from competing territorial claims, resource exploitation, and strategic interests among littoral states and global powers in the South China Sea.

The South China Sea is a strategically vital waterway through which trillions of dollars in trade flow annually, making it a focal point of geopolitical competition. Littoral states, including China, Vietnam, the Philippines, Malaysia, and Brunei, assert overlapping territorial claims, primarily cantered around the Spratly Islands, Paracel Islands, and Scarborough Shoal.

China's expansive claims, based on historical precedents and the Nine-Dash Line map, encroach upon the exclusive economic zones

(EEZs) of neighbouring countries and challenge the principles of freedom of navigation and international law. This assertiveness has sparked tensions with other claimants, notably Vietnam and the Philippines, as well as with non-claimant states like the United States, which maintains a presence in the region to uphold maritime security and ensure freedom of navigation.

The South China Sea is rich in natural resources, including oil, gas, fisheries, and minerals, making it a lucrative area for resource exploitation. Competing claims over these resources exacerbate geopolitical tensions and complicate efforts to resolve the dispute through diplomatic means.

The discovery of potential oil and gas reserves in disputed waters has heightened competition among claimant states and attracted the interest of international energy companies. Vietnam's exploration activities in areas claimed by China, as well as China's unilateral development of oil and gas fields in contested waters, have led to confrontations and diplomatic protests. Resource exploitation in the South China Sea thus becomes a source of both economic opportunity and geopolitical contention, fuelling rivalries among claimants and external actors.

The South China Sea is a vital maritime artery for global trade, with over one-third of global shipping passing through its waters. Concerns over China's assertive maritime claims and construction of artificial islands equipped with military facilities have raised alarms about the potential for conflict and disruptions to freedom of navigation.

The United States, as a major maritime power and advocate for freedom of navigation, conducts freedom of navigation operations (FONOPs) in the South China Sea to challenge what it perceives as excessive maritime claims that infringe upon international law. These operations, often involving the navigation of U.S. Navy ships within territorial waters claimed by China, aim to demonstrate the United States' commitment to upholding international norms and maritime security. However, such actions also risk escalating tensions and provoking responses from China, contributing to the militarization of the region.

Efforts to address the South China Sea dispute through multilateral diplomacy have been hindered by geopolitical rivalries and divergent interests among claimant states. Regional organizations such as the Association of Southeast Asian Nations (ASEAN) have sought to facilitate dialogue and confidence-building measures to manage tensions and prevent conflict.

The ASEAN-led framework for a Code of Conduct (COC) in the South China Sea exemplifies attempts to establish norms and rules of behaviour among claimant states. However, progress on the COC has been slow, with disagreements over its scope, enforceability, and mechanisms for dispute resolution. Despite challenges, diplomatic initiatives like the COC remain essential for reducing tensions, promoting dialogue, and maintaining regional stability in the South China Sea.

As littoral states and global powers vie for influence and control in the South China Sea, it is imperative to prioritize diplomatic solutions, uphold international law, and promote cooperation to ensure maritime security and regional stability. By fostering dialogue, respecting the rights of all stakeholders, and adhering to the principles of freedom of navigation and peaceful dispute resolution, the South China Sea can be managed as a shared resource for the benefit of all nations in the region.

Cyber-security and Geopolitics:

Navigating the Digital Frontier

The analysis of "Cyber-security and Geopolitics: Navigating the Digital Frontier" delves into the increasingly critical intersection between cyber-security and geopolitics, shedding light on how cyber capabilities and vulnerabilities shape global power dynamics, international relations, and national security strategies.

In an increasingly interconnected world, cyberspace has emerged as a new frontier for geopolitical competition and conflict. Cyber threats, including cyber espionage, sabotage, and warfare, pose significant challenges to governments, businesses, and individuals, highlighting the need for robust cyber-security measures and international cooperation.

Cyber-attacks attributed to state-sponsored actors, such as the alleged Russian interference in the 2016 U.S. presidential election and the SolarWinds supply chain attack, underscore the potential for cyber capabilities to disrupt democratic processes, compromise critical infrastructure, and undermine national security.

These incidents demonstrate how cyberspace has become a battleground for geopolitical rivalries, where states leverage digital tools to advance their strategic interests and exert influence on the global stage.

Cyber capabilities have become integral to modern warfare and intelligence operations, enabling states to conduct clandestine activities and exert coercive influence without resorting to traditional military force. The strategic use of cyber tools and techniques shapes the balance of power in international relations and influences the dynamics of conflict and cooperation.

The Stuxnet cyber-attack on Iran's nuclear program, reportedly orchestrated by the United States and Israel, exemplifies the strategic implications of cyber power. By exploiting vulnerabilities in Iran's industrial control systems, the attack disrupted uranium enrichment processes, delaying Iran's nuclear ambitions and demonstrating the potential of cyber weapons to achieve strategic objectives. Such covert operations blur the lines between warfare and espionage, challenging traditional notions of sovereignty and security in the digital age.

Cyber threats also pose significant risks to economic stability and competitiveness, as businesses and critical infrastructure systems increasingly rely on digital technologies for operations and communication. Cyber-attacks targeting financial institutions, energy grids, and supply chains can have far-reaching consequences for global economies and trade networks.

The WannaCry ransomware attack, which affected hundreds of thousands of computers worldwide in 2017, disrupted business operations, caused financial losses, and highlighted vulnerabilities in cyber-security defences. Similarly, the NotPetya cyber-attack, attributed to Russian state-sponsored actors, targeted Ukrainian infrastructure but had collateral damage on companies globally, including major multinational corporations. These incidents underscore the interconnected nature of cyber threats and the need for collective action to strengthen cyber-security resilience and mitigate economic risks.

Efforts to establish norms of behaviour and rules of engagement in cyberspace have become increasingly important in mitigating cyber risks and preventing escalation of conflicts. International forums and diplomatic initiatives seek to promote responsible state behaviour, protect human rights online, and address challenges of attribution and accountability in cyberspace.

The United Nations Group of Governmental Experts (UNGGE) on Developments in the Field of Information and Telecommunications in the Context of International Security has played a key role in advancing cyber-security norms at the international level. Agreements such as the Tallinn Manual, which provides guidance on the application of international law to cyber operations, contribute to the development of norms and standards for responsible state behaviour in cyberspace. These diplomatic efforts aim to build trust, foster cooperation, and reduce the risk of conflict in the digital domain.

As cyberspace becomes increasingly central to political, economic, and military activities, it is essential for states to prioritize cyber-security resilience, uphold international norms, and engage in diplomatic dialogue to address cyber threats effectively. By promoting cooperation, transparency, and responsible behaviour in cyberspace, the international community can navigate the digital frontier and mitigate the risks posed by cyber insecurity to global stability and security.

Climate Change and Geopolitics:

Navigating Environmental Challenges

The exploration of "Climate Change and Geopolitics: Navigating Environmental Challenges" delves into the intricate interplay between climate change and global geopolitics, emphasizing how environmental factors shape international relations, resource competition, and security dynamics.

Climate change, driven by human activities such as greenhouse gas emissions and deforestation, poses one of the most significant challenges to global security and stability. Rising temperatures, sea-level rise, extreme weather events, and shifts in precipitation patterns have far-reaching impacts on ecosystems, economies, and societies worldwide.

The melting of polar ice caps, such as those in the Arctic and Antarctic regions, has profound implications for global sea levels, coastal communities, and maritime transportation routes. As ice melts, it not only threatens the livelihoods of indigenous peoples and wildlife but also opens up new opportunities for resource extraction, shipping, and strategic military positioning. The Arctic, in particular, has become a focal point of geopolitical competition as melting ice exposes new shipping lanes and resource-rich territories.

Climate change exacerbates resource scarcity, particularly with regard to water, food, and arable land, leading to competition and conflicts over access and control. Vulnerable regions, such as the Sahel in Africa and the Middle East, face heightened risks of instability, mass migration, and humanitarian crises due to environmental degradation and resource depletion.

The Syrian civil war, often cited as an example of a "climate conflict," was precipitated by a combination of environmental stressors, socio-economic grievances, and political instability. Prolonged droughts and water shortages exacerbated by climate change contributed to agricultural failures, rural-to-urban migration, and social unrest, exacerbating tensions and triggering violent conflict. The Syrian case underscores the interconnectedness of environmental factors, socio-economic conditions, and political dynamics in shaping conflict risks.

Climate change requires coordinated and cooperative responses at the national, regional, and global levels to mitigate emissions, adapt to impacts, and promote sustainable development. International agreements such as the Paris Agreement, aimed at limiting global warming to well below 2 degrees Celsius, represent efforts to address climate change through multilateral cooperation and shared responsibility.

The Paris Agreement, adopted in 2015 by nearly 200 countries, outlines commitments to reduce greenhouse gas emissions, enhance climate resilience, and mobilize financial resources for climate action. While the agreement represents a significant milestone in global climate governance, challenges remain in implementation, financing, and accountability. Additionally, geopolitical tensions, shifting political priorities, and differing national interests complicate efforts to achieve collective action on climate change, underscoring the need for sustained diplomatic engagement and political leadership.

Climate change intersects with traditional security concerns, including energy security, food security, and human security, amplifying risks of conflict, displacement, and instability. Climate-related disasters, such as hurricanes, floods, and droughts, can have cascading effects on social cohesion, economic development, and political stability, particularly in vulnerable regions.

Small island states in the Pacific, such as Tuvalu and Kiribati, face existential threats from sea-level rise and coastal erosion, forcing governments to grapple with questions of sovereignty, migration, and adaptation. The plight of these nations has galvanized international attention and sparked discussions on climate-induced displacement, environmental justice, and the need for innovative solutions to address the human impacts of climate change. Climate diplomacy thus becomes crucial in fostering cooperation, resilience, and solidarity among nations facing shared climate challenges.

As the impacts of climate change intensify, it is imperative for nations to prioritize climate action, promote sustainable development, and strengthen resilience to mitigate risks and build a more secure and sustainable future for all. By recognizing the interconnectedness of environmental, social, and political factors, the international community can navigate the challenges of climate change and forge pathways to a more equitable and resilient world.

Geopolitical Implications of

Artificial Intelligence:

Shaping the Future Landscape

The analysis of "Geopolitical Implications of Artificial Intelligence: Shaping the Future Landscape" explores the transformative potential of artificial intelligence (AI) and its profound implications for global geopolitics, security, and governance. This examination sheds light on how advancements in AI technologies are reshaping traditional power structures, economic competitiveness, and strategic interests among nations.

Artificial intelligence has emerged as a strategic technology with wide-ranging applications across various sectors, including defence, healthcare, finance, and transportation. AI-driven innovations, such as autonomous weapons systems, predictive analytics, and intelligent automation, have the potential to revolutionize military capabilities, economic productivity, and societal development.

The development of autonomous drones and unmanned aerial vehicles (UAVs) equipped with AI algorithms enables precise targeting, reconnaissance, and surveillance capabilities in military operations. Nations investing in AI-powered defence systems seek to enhance situational awareness, decision-making speed, and operational efficiency, thereby gaining strategic advantages in conflict scenarios. The proliferation of AI technologies in defence highlights the growing importance of technological superiority in modern warfare and defence strategies.

AI innovation and adoption are increasingly viewed as essential drivers of economic competitiveness and technological leadership in the global arena. Countries and companies investing in AI research, development, and talent acquisition seek to harness the transformative potential of AI to drive economic growth, productivity gains, and job creation.

China's ambitious AI strategy, outlined in documents such as the "New Generation Artificial Intelligence Development Plan," aims to position the country as a global AI powerhouse by 2030. Through substantial investments in AI research institutes, talent cultivation programs, and strategic partnerships with industry leaders, China seeks to lead the AI race and establish dominance in key AI-driven industries, such as robotics, autonomous vehicles, and digital services. The pursuit of AI-driven economic competitiveness underscores the strategic imperative of technological innovation and talent development in the 21st-century global economy.

The rapid advancement of AI technologies raises ethical and regulatory challenges related to privacy, data protection, algorithmic bias, and accountability. Concerns about the misuse of AI for surveillance, manipulation, and social control underscore the need for robust governance frameworks and ethical guidelines to ensure the responsible development and deployment of AI systems.

The European Union's General Data Protection Regulation (GDPR) and emerging AI regulatory initiatives, such as the EU's proposed Artificial Intelligence Act, seek to establish clear rules and standards for the ethical use of AI. These regulations aim to safeguard individual rights, promote transparency and accountability in AI systems, and mitigate risks associated with algorithmic discrimination and unintended consequences. The adoption of ethical principles and regulatory measures reflects growing awareness of the societal impacts of AI and the importance of ethical considerations in AI governance.

AI-driven technological competition is reshaping geopolitical dynamics and strategic alliances among nations. The race for AI dominance and technological supremacy fuels rivalries among major powers, such as the United States, China, and Russia, while also prompting collaboration and knowledge-sharing initiatives to address common challenges and opportunities.

The U.S.-China AI competition often referred to as the "AI arms race," highlights the strategic implications of AI advancements for global power dynamics. Both countries invest heavily in AI research, development, and applications, with a focus on military applications, economic innovation, and technological leadership. At the same time, international initiatives, such as the

Global Partnership on Artificial Intelligence (GPAI) and the OECD AI Policy Observatory, facilitate dialogue, cooperation, and capacity-building efforts to promote AI governance, ethics, and best practices on a global scale. Balancing competitive interests with cooperative endeavours remains essential in navigating the evolving landscape of AI geopolitics.

"Geopolitical Implications of Artificial Intelligence: Shaping the Future Landscape" underscores the transformative potential of AI technologies and their far-reaching implications for global geopolitics, security, and governance. As nations navigate the opportunities and challenges presented by AI-driven innovation, it is essential to prioritize ethical considerations, regulatory frameworks, and international cooperation to harness the benefits of AI while mitigating risks and ensuring responsible and inclusive development. By fostering collaboration, transparency, and ethical leadership in AI governance, the international community can shape a future where AI technologies contribute to peace, prosperity, and human well-being on a global scale.

Renewable Energy and Geopolitics:

Shifting Power Dynamics in the Energy Landscape

The analysis of "Renewable Energy and Geopolitics: Shifting Power Dynamics in the Energy Landscape" explores the intersection of renewable energy development and global geopolitics, highlighting how the transition to renewable energy sources is reshaping traditional energy dynamics, geopolitical alliances, and strategic interests among nations.

Renewable energy sources, such as solar, wind, hydroelectric, and geothermal power, have gained prominence as viable alternatives to fossil fuels in addressing climate change and energy security concerns. The declining costs of renewable technologies, coupled with growing environmental awareness and policy support, have accelerated the transition to clean energy worldwide.

The rapid expansion of solar and wind energy capacity, particularly in countries like China, the United States, and Germany, underscores the global momentum towards renewable energy adoption. Solar photovoltaic (PV) and onshore/offshore wind installations have reached record levels, driven by advancements in technology, economies of scale, and favourable government policies. This shift towards renewables reflects a broader recognition of the environmental, economic, and geopolitical benefits of transitioning away from fossil fuels.

Renewable energy offers opportunities for enhanced energy independence and security by reducing reliance on imported fossil fuels and mitigating geopolitical risks associated with energy dependence. Countries investing in domestic renewable energy production seek to strengthen their energy resilience, diversify their energy portfolios, and reduce vulnerability to supply disruptions and price fluctuations in global energy markets.

Germany's Energiewende, or energy transition, exemplifies efforts to achieve energy independence and security through renewable energy deployment. By prioritizing investments in wind, solar, and biomass energy, Germany aims to reduce its reliance on fossil fuel imports, enhance energy self-sufficiency, and meet ambitious climate targets. Similarly, countries in the Middle East and North Africa region, endowed with abundant solar resources, are investing in large-scale solar energy projects to capitalize on their natural advantages and diversify their economies away from oil dependency.

The transition to renewable energy has geopolitical implications for energy-producing and energy-consuming nations, as well as for regions historically dependent on fossil fuel exports. Shifts in energy supply chains, market dynamics, and investment patterns reshape geopolitical alliances, influence economic competitiveness, and redefine strategic interests in the global energy landscape.

The decline of fossil fuel markets and the rise of renewable energy sources challenge the geopolitical dominance of traditional energy exporters, such as Russia, Saudi Arabia, and Venezuela. These countries face the prospect of diminishing revenues from oil and gas exports, which may undermine their geopolitical influence and economic stability. Conversely, countries leading in renewable energy innovation and production, such as China and the European Union, gain geopolitical leverage and soft power by exporting clean energy technologies and expertise to emerging markets.

Renewable energy fosters opportunities for climate diplomacy and international cooperation in addressing shared environmental challenges. Multilateral initiatives, such as the Paris Agreement and the United Nations Framework Convention on Climate Change (UNFCCC), provide platforms for dialogue, collaboration, and capacity-building efforts to accelerate the transition to renewable energy and mitigate climate change impacts.

Detailed Explanation: The International Solar Alliance (ISA), launched by India and France at the 2015 UN Climate Change Conference (COP21) in Paris, aims to promote solar energy deployment and facilitate technology transfer among solar-rich countries. By mobilizing political will and financial resources, the ISA fosters South-South cooperation and North-South partnerships in scaling up renewable energy investments and achieving sustainable development goals. Climate diplomacy initiatives like the ISA demonstrate the potential for renewable energy to serve as a catalyst for global cooperation and collective action in addressing the existential threat of climate change.

"Renewable Energy and Geopolitics: Shifting Power Dynamics in the Energy Landscape" underscores the transformative potential of renewable energy in reshaping global geopolitics, energy security, and climate governance. As nation's transition towards cleaner and more sustainable energy systems, it is imperative to prioritize collaboration, innovation, and inclusive development to realize the full benefits of renewable energy for all. By leveraging renewable energy as a catalyst for peace, prosperity, and environmental stewardship, the international community can navigate the complex geopolitics of energy transition and build a more resilient and sustainable future for generations to come.

Space Exploration and Geopolitics:

The New Frontier

The analysis of "Space Exploration and Geopolitics: The New Frontier" delves into the evolving landscape of space exploration and its profound implications for global geopolitics, technological innovation, and strategic competition among nations. This examination sheds light on how advancements in space technology, satellite systems, and lunar exploration are reshaping traditional power dynamics and influencing strategic interests in the space domain.

Space exploration has entered a new era of competition and collaboration, with governments, private companies, and international consortia vying for leadership and influence in space activities. The resurgence of interest in lunar exploration, Mars missions, and commercial space ventures has fuelled a renewed space race characterized by technological innovation, investment mobilization, and geopolitical rivalry.

The Artemis program, led by NASA, aims to return humans to the Moon by 2024 and establish a sustainable lunar presence as a stepping stone for future Mars missions. Concurrently, other spacefaring nations, including China, Russia, and India, are pursuing ambitious lunar exploration plans, signalling a renaissance of interest in space exploration beyond Earth's orbit. Moreover, the emergence of private space companies like SpaceX, Blue Origin, and Virgin Galactic disrupt traditional space paradigms, challenging government monopolies and catalysing commercialization of space activities.

Satellite systems and space infrastructure play critical roles in modern warfare, intelligence operations, telecommunications, and global navigation systems. Nations with advanced space capabilities leverage satellites for military reconnaissance, communication networks, and positioning, navigation, and timing (PNT) services, enhancing their strategic advantages and national security postures.

The United States' Global Positioning System (GPS), comprised of a constellation of satellites orbiting Earth, provides precise timing and location information for military, civilian, and commercial users worldwide. GPS-enabled navigation and targeting systems empower military forces to conduct precision strikes, reconnaissance missions, and logistics operations with unprecedented accuracy and efficiency. Similarly, satellite communication networks enable real-time data transmission, command, and control capabilities for military and intelligence agencies, enhancing situational awareness and decision-making in conflict scenarios.

The commercialization of space activities, driven by private sector investments and entrepreneurial ventures, opens up new opportunities for economic growth, innovation, and international collaboration. Commercial space ventures, such as satellite launches, space tourism, asteroid mining, and in-orbit servicing, disrupt traditional space industries and create new markets and business opportunities.

SpaceX's reusable rocket technology and ambitious Starlink satellite constellation project exemplify the commercialization of space and the democratization of access to space. By lowering launch costs and increasing launch frequency, SpaceX revolutionizes the space launch market, attracting customers from government agencies, commercial enterprises, and international partners. Moreover, the burgeoning space tourism industry, led by companies like Blue Origin and Virgin Galactic, offers civilians the opportunity to experience space travel and contribute to the commercialization of low Earth orbit (LEO) activities.

As space activities proliferate and space debris accumulates in Earth's orbit, the need for robust space governance mechanisms and international cooperation becomes increasingly urgent. Multilateral agreements, space treaties, and regulatory frameworks govern space exploration, satellite operations, and space debris mitigation, promoting responsible behaviour, transparency, and sustainability in the space domain.

The Outer Space Treaty, ratified by over 100 countries, establishes principles for the peaceful use of outer space, prohibits the placement of weapons of mass destruction in space, and promotes international cooperation in space exploration and scientific research. Additionally, organizations like the United Nations Office for Outer Space Affairs (UNOOSA) facilitate dialogue, capacity-building, and information sharing among spacefaring nations to address common challenges and promote best practices in space governance. Strengthening international cooperation and adherence to space law principles are essential in ensuring the long-term sustainability and security of outer space activities.

As nations navigate the complexities of space activities, it is imperative to prioritize international cooperation, responsible stewardship, and equitable access to space for the benefit of all humankind. By fostering collaboration, transparency, and innovation in space exploration, the international community can unlock the full potential of the space domain and advance collective aspirations for exploration, discovery, and peaceful cooperation in the cosmos.

Blockchain Technology and Geopolitics:

Transforming Trust and Security

The examination of "Blockchain Technology and Geopolitics: Transforming Trust and Security" explores the disruptive potential of blockchain technology and its profound implications for global geopolitics, security, and governance. This analysis sheds light on how blockchain innovations, such as decentralized ledgers, smart contracts, and digital currencies, are reshaping traditional power structures, economic systems, and international relations.

Blockchain technology enables decentralized trust mechanisms through cryptographic protocols, consensus algorithms, and distributed ledger systems. By removing the need for intermediaries and central authorities, blockchain networks facilitate peer-to-peer transactions, data verification, and secure record-keeping, enhancing trust, transparency, and security in digital interactions.

Bitcoin, the first decentralized crypto-currency powered by blockchain technology, enables peer-to-peer electronic payments without relying on banks or financial institutions. Transactions on the Bitcoin blockchain are validated and recorded by a decentralized network of nodes, ensuring transparency and immutability of transaction history. Similarly, blockchain-based identity management systems, such as Self-Sovereign Identity (SSI), empower individuals to control their digital identities and authenticate personal information without relying on centralized databases or third-party verifiers.

Blockchain technology disrupts traditional financial systems and intermediaries by enabling borderless, frictionless, and programmable value transfer. Crypto-currencies, tokenized assets, and decentralized finance (DeFi) platforms democratize access to financial services, promote financial inclusion, and empower underserved populations to participate in the global economy.

DeFi platforms, built on blockchain networks like Ethereum, facilitate decentralized lending, borrowing, trading, and asset management without intermediaries or centralized exchanges. Users can access financial services, earn yields, and manage digital assets through smart contracts, automated protocols, and decentralized applications (DApps). Moreover, blockchain-based remittance services, such as Ripple's XRP, offer low-cost, instant cross-border payments, disrupting traditional remittance channels and reducing reliance on legacy banking systems.

Crypto-currencies and central bank digital currencies (CBDCs) challenge the dominance of sovereign currencies and traditional monetary systems, raising concerns about monetary sovereignty, financial stability, and regulatory oversight. Governments and central banks grapple with the regulatory and security challenges posed by digital currencies, balancing innovation with consumer protection and national security interests.

China's digital yuan initiative, piloted by the People's Bank of China (PBOC), aims to digitize the national currency and establish a sovereign digital currency ecosystem. The digital yuan, built on a centralized blockchain infrastructure, enables the PBOC to monitor and control monetary flows, combat financial crimes, and enhance monetary policy effectiveness. Conversely, decentralized crypto-currencies like Bitcoin and Ethereum challenge centralized monetary authorities and traditional banking systems, advocating for financial autonomy, censorship resistance, and privacy protection.

Blockchain technology fosters opportunities for blockchain diplomacy, cross-border cooperation, and public-private partnerships in addressing global challenges and advancing shared goals. Multilateral initiatives, standardization efforts, and blockchain consortia promote interoperability, scalability, and sustainability of blockchain solutions across diverse sectors and regions.

The World Economic Forum's Global Blockchain Council and the United Nations' Blockchain for Impact initiative convene stakeholders from governments, academia, industry, and civil society to explore blockchain applications for sustainable development, humanitarian aid, and environmental conservation. Moreover, international blockchain consortia, such as the Enterprise Ethereum Alliance and the Hyperledger Foundation, develop open-source blockchain protocols and industry standards to facilitate collaboration and innovation in blockchain ecosystems. By fostering dialogue, collaboration, and knowledge-sharing, blockchain diplomacy initiatives promote inclusive and equitable deployment of blockchain technologies for societal benefit.

As nations navigate the opportunities and challenges presented by blockchain innovations, it is imperative to prioritize collaboration, regulation, and responsible governance to harness the benefits of blockchain while mitigating risks and ensuring inclusivity and sustainability. By fostering an enabling environment for blockchain adoption and fostering international cooperation, the international community can unlock the full potential of blockchain technology to advance trust, security, and prosperity in the digital age.

Biotechnology and Geopolitics:

Redefining Health and Security

The analysis of "Biotechnology and Geopolitics: Redefining Health and Security" delves into the transformative impact of biotechnology on global geopolitics, health systems, and security paradigms. This examination highlights how advancements in biotechnology, including gene editing, synthetic biology, and biopharmaceuticals, are reshaping traditional power dynamics, public health strategies, and international relations.

Biotechnology innovations hold immense potential for addressing global health challenges, including infectious diseases, pandemics, and bioterrorism threats. Breakthroughs in vaccine development, diagnostic technologies, and genomic sequencing empower healthcare systems to detect, prevent, and respond to emerging health threats with greater precision and speed.

The development of mRNA vaccines, such as those against COVID-19, exemplifies the transformative impact of biotechnology on pandemic response efforts. mRNA vaccines, like those produced by Pfizer-BioNTech and Moderna, leverage genetic engineering techniques to induce immune responses against viral pathogens, offering unprecedented efficacy and scalability in vaccine production. Similarly, advances in rapid diagnostic tests, CRISPR-based gene editing, and monoclonal antibody therapies enhance the arsenal of tools available for combating infectious diseases and ensuring global health security.

The proliferation of genetic engineering technologies raises concerns about biosecurity risks, dual-use applications, and ethical considerations in biotechnology research and development. Gene editing tools like CRISPR-Cas9 enable precise manipulation of genetic material, presenting opportunities for medical breakthroughs and agricultural innovations but also posing risks of unintended consequences and bioterrorism threats.

The potential misuse of gene editing technologies for bioweapons development and biological warfare underscores the importance of robust biosecurity measures and ethical oversight in biotechnology research. International agreements, such as the Biological Weapons Convention (BWC), aim to prevent the proliferation of biological weapons and ensure responsible conduct in life sciences research. Additionally, initiatives like the Global Health Security Agenda (GHSA) promote collaboration, capacity-building, and information-sharing among nations to strengthen pandemic preparedness and response capabilities.

Biopharmaceutical innovation and drug development play pivotal roles in advancing public health, economic prosperity, and diplomatic relations among nations. Access to life-saving medicines, vaccines, and medical technologies becomes a key determinant of health outcomes and socio-economic development, shaping geopolitical alliances and global health diplomacy efforts.

The COVAX initiative, co-led by the World Health Organization (WHO), Gavi, and the Coalition for Epidemic Preparedness Innovations (CEPI), aims to ensure equitable access to COVID-19 vaccines for all countries, regardless of income levels. COVAX facilitates vaccine procurement, distribution, and deployment to low- and middle-income countries, promoting solidarity and shared responsibility in global pandemic response efforts. Moreover, public-private partnerships, such as the Access to COVID-19 Tools Accelerator (ACT-Accelerator), mobilize resources and expertise from governments, philanthropic organizations, and pharmaceutical companies to accelerate vaccine development and ensure equitable access to diagnostics, treatments, and vaccines for COVID-19 and other health threats.

Biotechnology raises complex ethical, legal, and social implications related to genetic privacy, human enhancement, and bioethics. Debates surrounding genome editing, stem cell research, and reproductive technologies highlight the need for ethical guidelines, regulatory frameworks, and public engagement in shaping biotechnological governance and responsible innovation.

The UNESCO Universal Declaration on Bioethics and Human Rights provides principles and guidelines for ethical conduct in life sciences research and biotechnological applications.

These principles emphasize respect for human dignity, autonomy, and informed consent in biomedicine and biotechnology, balancing scientific progress with societal values and human rights. Additionally, regulatory agencies like the U.S. Food and Drug Administration (FDA) and the European Medicines Agency (EMA) enforce safety standards and ethical requirements for biopharmaceutical products, ensuring patient safety and public trust in biotechnological innovations.

As nations navigate the opportunities and challenges presented by biotechnological advancements, it is imperative to prioritize collaboration, transparency, and ethical governance to harness the benefits of biotechnology while mitigating risks and ensuring equitable access to life-saving innovations. By fostering international cooperation and ethical leadership in biotechnological research and development, the global community can advance health equity, security, and resilience in an increasingly interconnected world.

Renewable Energy and Geopolitics:

Shifting Power Dynamics in the Energy Landscape

The analysis of "Renewable Energy and Geopolitics: Shifting Power Dynamics in the Energy Landscape" explores the intersection of renewable energy development and global geopolitics, highlighting how the transition to renewable energy sources is reshaping traditional energy dynamics, geopolitical alliances, and strategic interests among nations.

Renewable energy sources, such as solar, wind, hydroelectric, and geothermal power, have gained prominence as viable alternatives to fossil fuels in addressing climate change and energy security concerns. The declining costs of renewable technologies, coupled with growing environmental awareness and policy support, have accelerated the transition to clean energy worldwide.

The rapid expansion of solar and wind energy capacity, particularly in countries like China, the United States, and Germany, underscores the global momentum towards renewable energy adoption. Solar photovoltaic (PV) and onshore/offshore wind installations have reached record levels, driven by advancements in technology, economies of scale, and favourable government policies. This shift towards renewables reflects a broader recognition of the environmental, economic, and geopolitical benefits of transitioning away from fossil fuels.

Renewable energy offers opportunities for enhanced energy independence and security by reducing reliance on imported fossil fuels and mitigating geopolitical risks associated with energy dependence. Countries investing in domestic renewable energy production seek to strengthen their energy resilience, diversify their energy portfolios, and reduce vulnerability to supply disruptions and price fluctuations in global energy markets.

Germany's Energiewende, or energy transition, exemplifies efforts to achieve energy independence and security through renewable energy deployment. By prioritizing investments in wind, solar, and biomass energy, Germany aims to reduce its reliance on fossil fuel imports, enhance energy self-sufficiency, and meet ambitious climate targets. Similarly, countries in the Middle East and North Africa region, endowed with abundant solar resources, are investing in large-scale solar energy projects to capitalize on their natural advantages and diversify their economies away from oil dependency.

The transition to renewable energy has geopolitical implications for energy-producing and energy-consuming nations, as well as for regions historically dependent on fossil fuel exports. Shifts in energy supply chains, market dynamics, and investment patterns reshape geopolitical alliances, influence economic competitiveness, and redefine strategic interests in the global energy landscape.

The decline of fossil fuel markets and the rise of renewable energy sources challenge the geopolitical dominance of traditional energy exporters, such as Russia, Saudi Arabia, and Venezuela. These countries face the prospect of diminishing revenues from oil and gas exports, which may undermine their geopolitical influence and economic stability. Conversely, countries leading in renewable energy innovation and production, such as China and the European Union, gain geopolitical leverage and soft power by exporting clean energy technologies and expertise to emerging markets.

Renewable energy fosters opportunities for climate diplomacy and international cooperation in addressing shared environmental challenges. Multilateral initiatives, such as the Paris Agreement and the United Nations Framework Convention on Climate Change (UNFCCC), provide platforms for dialogue, collaboration, and capacity-building efforts to accelerate the transition to renewable energy and mitigate climate change impacts.

The International Solar Alliance (ISA), launched by India and France at the 2015 UN Climate Change Conference (COP21) in Paris, aims to promote solar energy deployment and facilitate technology transfer among solar-rich countries. By mobilizing political will and financial resources, the ISA fosters South-South cooperation and North-South partnerships in scaling up renewable energy investments and achieving sustainable development goals.

Climate diplomacy initiatives like the ISA demonstrate the potential for renewable energy to serve as a catalyst for global cooperation and collective action in addressing the existential threat of climate change.

As nations navigate towards cleaner and more sustainable energy systems, it is imperative to prioritize collaboration, innovation, and inclusive development to realize the full benefits of renewable energy for all. By fostering cooperation, transparency, and ethical leadership in renewable energy governance, the international community can unlock the full potential of renewable energy to advance peace, prosperity, and environmental sustainability on a global scale.

Cyber-security and Geopolitics:

Securing the Digital Frontier

The analysis of "Cyber-security and Geopolitics: Securing the Digital Frontier" delves into the evolving landscape of cyber-security and its profound implications for global geopolitics, national security, and international relations. This examination highlights how advancements in cyberspace technologies, digital infrastructure, and cyber warfare capabilities are reshaping traditional power dynamics and influencing strategic interests among nations.

The proliferation of digital technologies and interconnected systems has led to an increase in cyber threats, including cyber-attacks, data breaches, and information warfare campaigns. State and non-state actors exploit vulnerabilities in digital networks to disrupt critical infrastructure, steal sensitive information, and undermine trust in democratic institutions, posing significant challenges to national security and international stability.

Cyber-attacks targeting critical infrastructure, such as power grids, transportation networks, and financial systems, pose serious risks to public safety, economic stability, and national security. Nation-state adversaries like Russia, China, and North Korea, leverage sophisticated cyber capabilities to conduct espionage, sabotage, and influence operations against rival nations and strategic adversaries. Moreover, non-state actors, including criminal organizations and hacktivist groups, exploit cyber vulnerabilities to perpetrate cybercrime, ransomware attacks, and dIsInformation campaigns for financial gain or ideological motives.

Cyber warfare capabilities and offensive cyber operations have become integral components of modern military strategies and geopolitical competition. Nations invest in cyber defence, cyber espionage, and offensive cyber capabilities to protect national interests, project power in cyberspace, and deter adversaries from hostile actions in the digital domain.

The United States' Cyber Command and China's Strategic Support Force exemplify the integration of cyber warfare capabilities into national defence structures and military doctrines. These specialized cyber units conduct offensive cyber operations, defensive cyber measures, and intelligence gathering activities to safeguard national security interests and maintain strategic advantage in cyberspace. Moreover, the emergence of cyber proxies and cyber mercenaries, sponsored by state actors or criminal organizations, further complicates the attribution and escalation of cyber conflicts, blurring the lines between state-sponsored cyber operations and cybercrime activities.

Cyber-security cooperation, cyber diplomacy, and the development of international norms and rules of behaviour in cyberspace are essential for mitigating cyber threats, promoting stability, and fostering trust among nations. Multilateral initiatives, such as the United Nations Group of Governmental Experts (UN GGE) and the Budapest Convention on Cybercrime, facilitate dialogue, capacity-building, and information-sharing efforts to address common cyber-security challenges and promote responsible state behaviour in cyberspace.

The Tallinn Manual, produced by an independent group of legal experts, offers guidance on the interpretation of international law in cyberspace and the applicability of existing legal frameworks to cyber operations. Additionally, cyber-security alliances and information-sharing mechanisms, like the Five Eyes intelligence alliance and the NATO Cooperative Cyber Defence Centre of Excellence (CCDCOE), enhance collaboration and coordination among like-minded nations in detecting, attributing, and responding to cyber threats. By promoting transparency, accountability, and adherence to agreed-upon norms and principles, cyber diplomacy initiatives contribute to enhancing cyber resilience and reducing the risk of cyber conflicts.

Cyber-security plays a critical role in safeguarding economic resilience, digital infrastructure, and supply chain integrity against cyber threats and disruptions. Cyber resilience measures, including cyber-security standards, incident response protocols, and risk management frameworks, help organizations and governments mitigate cyber risks, protect critical assets, and ensure business continuity in an increasingly interconnected and digitized world.

The SolarWinds cyber-attack, attributed to Russian state-sponsored actors, underscores the vulnerabilities in global supply chains and the interconnectedness of digital ecosystems. The compromise of SolarWinds' software supply chain resulted in widespread cyber espionage and data breaches affecting government agencies, technology firms, and critical infrastructure operators. In response, governments and private sector organizations prioritize supply chain security, threat intelligence sharing, and cyber resilience investments to detect, prevent, and mitigate supply chain attacks and cyber incidents.

As nations navigate the complexities of cyber-security challenges, it is imperative to prioritize cooperation, resilience, and responsible state behaviour to mitigate cyber risks and build a safer, more secure digital future. By fostering collaboration, transparency, and adherence to agreed-upon norms and principles, the international community can enhance cyber-security resilience and preserve peace and stability in the digital age.

Artificial Intelligence and Geopolitics:

Shaping the Future Landscape

The analysis of "Artificial Intelligence and Geopolitics: Shaping the Future Landscape" explores the transformative potential of artificial intelligence (AI) and its profound implications for global geopolitics, security, and governance. This examination sheds light on how advancements in AI technologies, including machine learning, natural language processing, and autonomous systems, are reshaping traditional power dynamics, economic competitiveness, and strategic interests among nations.

Artificial intelligence has emerged as a strategic technology with wide-ranging applications across various sectors, including defence, healthcare, finance, and transportation. AI-driven innovations, such as autonomous weapons systems, predictive analytics, and intelligent automation, have the potential to revolutionize military capabilities, economic productivity, and societal development.

The development of autonomous drones and unmanned aerial vehicles (UAVs) equipped with

AI algorithms enables precise targeting, reconnaissance, and surveillance capabilities in military operations. Nations investing in AI-powered defence systems seek to enhance situational awareness, decision-making speed, and operational efficiency, thereby gaining strategic advantages in conflict scenarios. The proliferation of AI technologies in defence highlights the growing importance of technological superiority in modern warfare and defence strategies.

AI innovation and adoption are increasingly viewed as essential drivers of economic competitiveness and technological leadership in the global arena. Countries and companies investing in AI research, development, and talent acquisition seek to harness the transformative potential of AI to drive economic growth, productivity gains, and job creation.

China's ambitious AI strategy, outlined in documents such as the "New Generation Artificial Intelligence Development Plan," aims to position the country as a global AI powerhouse by 2030. Through substantial investments in AI research institutes, talent cultivation programs, and strategic partnerships with industry leaders, China seeks to lead the AI race and establish dominance in key AI-driven industries, such as robotics, autonomous vehicles, and digital services. The pursuit of AI-driven economic competitiveness underscores the strategic imperative of technological innovation and talent development in the 21st-century global economy.

The rapid advancement of AI technologies raises ethical and regulatory challenges related to privacy, data protection, algorithmic bias, and accountability. Concerns about the misuse of AI for surveillance, manipulation, and social control underscore the need for robust governance frameworks and ethical guidelines to ensure the responsible development and deployment of AI systems.

The European Union's General Data Protection Regulation (GDPR) and emerging AI regulatory initiatives, such as the EU's proposed Artificial Intelligence Act, seek to establish clear rules and standards for the ethical use of AI. These regulations aim to safeguard individual rights, promote transparency and accountability in AI systems, and mitigate risks associated with algorithmic discrimination and unintended consequences. The adoption of ethical principles and regulatory measures reflects growing awareness of the societal impacts of AI and the importance of ethical considerations in AI governance.

AI-driven technological competition is reshaping geopolitical dynamics and strategic alliances among nations. The race for AI dominance and technological supremacy fuels rivalries among major powers, such as the United States, China, and Russia, while also prompting collaboration and knowledge-sharing initiatives to address common challenges and opportunities.

The U.S.-China AI competition often referred to as the "AI arms race," highlights the strategic implications of AI advancements for global power dynamics. Both countries invest heavily in AI research, development, and applications, with a focus on military applications, economic innovation, and technological leadership. At the same time, international initiatives, such as the Global Partnership on Artificial Intelligence (GPAI) and the OECD AI Policy Observatory, facilitate dialogue, cooperation, and capacity-building efforts to promote AI governance, ethics, and best practices on a global scale. Balancing competitive interests with cooperative endeavours remains essential in navigating the evolving landscape of AI geopolitics.

As nations navigate the opportunities and challenges presented by AI-driven innovation, it is essential to prioritize ethical considerations, regulatory frameworks, and international cooperation to harness the benefits of AI while mitigating risks and ensuring responsible and inclusive development. By fostering collaboration, transparency, and ethical leadership in AI governance, the international community can shape a future where AI technologies contribute to peace, prosperity, and human well-being on a global scale.

Exporting Values:

The Geopolitical Implications

of Promoting Democracy and Human Rights

The promotion of democracy and human rights has long been intertwined with geopolitical strategies and international relations. This endeavour, often termed "exporting values," carries significant implications for global politics, diplomacy, and security. In this essay, we delve into the multifaceted nature of promoting democracy and human rights on the international stage, examining the motivations, methods, and geopolitical implications associated with these efforts.

The promotion of democracy and human rights by powerful nations and international organizations is driven by a combination of altruistic, strategic, and self-interest motivations. Altruistically, the belief in the universality of human rights and democratic principles compels nations to advocate for their universal adoption and implementation. Democracies often view the spread of democratic governance and respect for human rights as essential for fostering global stability, prosperity, and peace.

For instance, the United States has historically positioned itself as a champion of democracy and human rights, promoting these values as integral to its foreign policy objectives. The promotion of democracy and human rights aligns with America's self-image as a beacon of freedom and democracy, fostering goodwill and soft power influence around the world. Similarly, international organizations like the United Nations and the European Union prioritize human rights promotion as part of their normative agendas, seeking to uphold global standards of human dignity and justice.

Strategically, the promotion of democracy and human rights serves as a means to advance national interests and geopolitical objectives. Democracies often perceive authoritarian regimes as threats to regional stability, security, and democratic norms, leading them to support democratization movements and civil society actors in autocratic states. By fostering democratic governance and respect for human rights, nations aim to create allies, counter adversaries, and expand their spheres of influence in strategically important regions.

The methods employed in promoting democracy and human rights vary depending on the geopolitical context, cultural considerations, and strategic imperatives of nations and organizations involved. Diplomatic pressure, economic incentives, foreign aid, and military interventions are among the tools used to advance democratic governance, civil liberties, and human rights protections worldwide.

Diplomatic pressure and multilateral sanctions are often deployed to condemn human rights abuses and authoritarian practices, signalling international disapproval and isolating oppressive regimes diplomatically. Economic incentives, such as trade agreements, foreign aid, and development assistance, are leveraged to incentivize democratic reforms and human rights improvements in recipient countries. Additionally, civil society support, democracy promotion programs, and capacity-building initiatives aim to strengthen democratic institutions, empower marginalized groups, and promote political participation and accountability.

In some cases, military interventions and peacekeeping operations are undertaken to protect civilian populations from human rights violations, restore democratic governance, and uphold international humanitarian law. However, the use of military force for humanitarian purposes is highly contentious and subject to scrutiny due to its potential for unintended consequences, civilian casualties, and geopolitical backlash.

The promotion of democracy and human rights carries significant geopolitical implications and challenges, shaping international relations, regional dynamics, and domestic politics in target countries and donor nations alike. Geopolitical competition, regime resistance, cultural relativism, and backlash against external interference pose formidable obstacles to the effectiveness and legitimacy of democracy promotion efforts.

Geopolitical competition between democratic and authoritarian powers, such as the United States and China, influences the success and scope of democracy promotion initiatives globally. Authoritarian regimes often resist external pressure to democratize, viewing democracy promotion as a threat to their stability, sovereignty, and legitimacy. Cultural relativism and divergent interpretations of human rights norms complicate efforts to promote universal standards of human rights and democratic governance, reflecting differences in historical, cultural, and religious contexts.

Furthermore, backlash against external interference and perceived Western imperialism fuels anti-democratic sentiments and nationalist movements in target countries, undermining democratization efforts and fostering geopolitical tensions. The Iraq War and the Arab Spring revolutions illustrate the complexities and unintended consequences of external interventions in promoting democracy and human rights, highlighting the need for context-specific approaches and nuanced strategies tailored to local conditions.

While the promotion of democracy and human rights reflects noble aspirations and universal principles, it also entails complex geopolitical calculations, strategic trade-offs, and ethical dilemmas. By recognizing the geopolitical implications and challenges associated with democracy promotion, nations and international organizations can adopt pragmatic, context-sensitive approaches that prioritize dialogue, partnership, and respect for sovereignty and self-determination. Ultimately, fostering a world characterized by democratic governance, human rights protections, and inclusive development requires sustained commitment, collaboration, and adaptation to the evolving dynamics of global politics and diplomacy.

Dollars and Dominance:

The Role of Currency in Geopolitical Strategy

The global financial system, with its intricate web of currencies, markets, and institutions, plays a central role in shaping geopolitical dynamics, power relations, and international stability. The dominance of certain currencies, notably the US dollar, exerts significant influence over economic policies, trade relations, and geopolitical alliances worldwide. In this essay, we explore the geopolitical implications of global financial systems, focusing on the role of currency in shaping geopolitical strategy and power dynamics on the international stage.

The US dollar has long served as the world's primary reserve currency, enjoying unparalleled dominance in global financial markets and trade transactions. The "petrodollar system," established in the 1970s, cemented the dollar's hegemonic status by linking oil trade with the currency, ensuring its widespread acceptance and demand. As a result, the US wields immense influence over the global economy and geopolitical affairs through its control over the dollar's issuance, monetary policy, and financial infrastructure.

The US dollar's status as the dominant reserve currency confers significant geopolitical advantages, including the ability to fund deficits, finance military expenditures, and project economic influence abroad. Moreover, the dollar's role as the primary medium of exchange for commodities, such as oil and gold, gives the US considerable leverage over energy markets and geopolitical dynamics in resource-rich regions like the Middle East. The dollar's centrality in international finance facilitates US financial sanctions, trade restrictions, and economic coercion against perceived adversaries, exerting coercive power and influence over global actors.

The pursuit of currency manipulation, exchange rate policies, and currency devaluation strategies is a common tactic employed by nations to gain competitive advantages in global trade, investment, and finance. Currency wars and economic rivalries exacerbate tensions between nations, fuelling geopolitical rivalries, trade disputes, and financial instability on the world stage.

China's management of its currency, the renminbi (RMB), provides a prominent example of currency manipulation as a tool of geopolitical strategy. China's intervention in foreign exchange markets, currency pegging practices, and capital controls aim to maintain export competitiveness, control capital flows, and preserve domestic economic stability. However, China's currency policies have drawn criticism from trading partners, particularly the United States, which accuses China of currency manipulation to gain unfair trade advantages and erode American competitiveness in global markets. Currency tensions between the US and China underscore the geopolitical dimensions of currency policies and their impact on bilateral relations and global economic governance.

The weaponization of finance and the use of economic statecraft as geopolitical tools pose significant challenges to global stability and security. Financial warfare encompasses a range of tactics, including economic sanctions, financial espionage, and cyber-attacks targeting financial systems, aimed at coercing or punishing adversaries and achieving strategic objectives.

The use of financial sanctions by the United States, particularly against Iran, Russia, and North Korea, demonstrates the effectiveness of financial instruments as tools of geopolitical coercion and influence. Sanctions targeting individuals, entities, and sectors of the economy aim to disrupt financial networks, constrain access to capital, and undermine economic stability, thereby exerting pressure on targeted regimes to change behaviour or face economic isolation. However, financial warfare also carries risks of unintended consequences, retaliatory measures, and collateral damage to innocent civilians, underscoring the ethical and strategic dilemmas inherent in economic statecraft.

The emergence of digital currencies, blockchain technology, and financial innovations poses new challenges and opportunities for global financial systems and geopolitical dynamics. Digital currencies, such as Bitcoin and central bank digital currencies (CBDCs), challenge the primacy of traditional fiat currencies and reshape the landscape of global finance, monetary policy, and economic governance.

China's development of a digital yuan, for instance, represents a strategic move to enhance financial sovereignty, reduce dependence on the US dollar, and establish digital payment systems that bypass Western financial infrastructure. The digital yuan could potentially undermine the dollar's dominance in international trade and finance, leading to shifts in geopolitical power and influence. Moreover, blockchain technology offers opportunities for financial inclusion, transparency, and efficiency, while also posing challenges to regulatory oversight, financial stability, and privacy protection.

As nations navigate the complexities of global financial systems, it is essential to recognize the geopolitical implications of currency policies, financial innovations, and economic rivalries. By fostering cooperation, transparency, and responsible governance in global finance, the international community can mitigate risks, promote stability, and ensure inclusive and sustainable development in an increasingly interconnected and digitized world.

Soft Power Strategies:

The Role of Cultural Diplomacy

in Shaping Geopolitical Landscapes

Cultural diplomacy, a cornerstone of soft power, has emerged as a pivotal instrument for nations seeking to wield influence, foster relationships, and advance their interests on the global stage. In this paper, we delve into the profound impact of cultural diplomacy on geopolitical landscapes, examining how nations utilize cultural assets, exchange programs, and cultural initiatives to bolster their soft power and geopolitical sway.

Soft power, a concept coined by political scientist Joseph Nye, refers to a nation's ability to influence others through attraction, persuasion, and cultural appeal, rather than coercion or force. Cultural diplomacy taps into this soft power by leveraging a nation's cultural heritage, arts, media, language, and values to cultivate goodwill, promote understanding, and strengthen connections with foreign audiences. By projecting a positive image and fostering affinity, nations can enhance their credibility, legitimacy, and influence in global affairs.

Soft power operates on the principle of attraction rather than coercion. It entails the ability of a nation to shape the preferences of others through the appeal of its culture, values, and policies. For example, Hollywood movies, American music, and British literature have contributed to shaping global perceptions of Western values and lifestyles, thereby exerting soft power influence on a global scale. Soft power enables nations to achieve their objectives by influencing the behaviour and attitudes of others through persuasive means, such as cultural exports, educational exchanges, and diplomatic initiatives.

Cultural Diplomacy in Practice: Cultural diplomacy encompasses a broad spectrum of activities, including cultural exchanges, artistic collaborations, educational programs, and public diplomacy initiatives. These endeavours aim to showcase a nation's cultural richness, diversity, and creativity, fostering mutual understanding, dialogue, and cooperation among nations. Cultural diplomacy initiatives, such as language immersion programs, film festivals, and cultural exhibitions, serve as platforms for intercultural dialogue, people-to-people exchanges, and grassroots engagement, thereby strengthening diplomatic ties and nurturing enduring relationships.

Cultural diplomacy manifests in various forms, each designed to foster mutual understanding and promote goodwill between nations. For instance, cultural exchanges involve the reciprocal sharing of artistic performances, exhibitions, and festivals to showcase a nation's cultural heritage and traditions. Educational programs, such as foreign language courses and academic exchanges, facilitate cross-cultural learning and academic collaboration, fostering personal connections and cross-border friendships. Public diplomacy initiatives, including cultural events, exhibitions, and cultural centres, aim to engage foreign audiences and shape perceptions of a nation's values, policies, and priorities.

China's proactive pursuit of cultural diplomacy represents a prominent example of leveraging soft power to bolster geopolitical influence and enhance public diplomacy efforts. Through initiatives like the Confucius Institute, which promotes Chinese language and culture abroad, and the Belt and Road Initiative (BRI), which fosters cultural exchanges and infrastructure development along ancient trade routes, China seeks to bolster its global image, expand its influence, and shape international perceptions of its rise as a global power. By investing in cultural infrastructure, media outlets, and educational exchanges, China aims to project a positive narrative of its civilization, values, and contributions to global development, thereby enhancing its soft power and geopolitical standing.

China's cultural diplomacy initiatives are part of a broader strategy to enhance its soft power and influence on the global stage. The Confucius Institute, established in partnership with foreign universities and cultural institutions, promotes Chinese language and culture through language courses, cultural events, and academic exchanges. By disseminating Chinese language and cultural knowledge, the Confucius Institute aims to foster mutual understanding and strengthen cultural ties between China and other nations. Similarly, the Belt and Road Initiative (BRI) integrates cultural diplomacy with economic development by promoting cultural exchanges, tourism, and people-to-people connections along the BRI routes. Through cultural diplomacy, China seeks to enhance its image, increase its soft power, and build relationships with countries participating in the BRI, thereby advancing its geopolitical interests and expanding its global influence.

Despite its potential benefits, cultural diplomacy faces challenges and controversies, including concerns about propaganda, censorship, and cultural imperialism. Nations often employ cultural diplomacy as a means of advancing political agendas and shaping international perceptions, raising questions about authenticity, representation, and power dynamics in cultural exchanges. Moreover, cultural diplomacy initiatives may inadvertently reinforce stereotypes, perpetuate inequalities, or exacerbate cultural conflicts, highlighting the need for ethical guidelines, diversity, and inclusivity in cultural exchange programs.

Cultural diplomacy is not without its limitations and ethical considerations. Governments may exploit cultural diplomacy initiatives for propaganda purposes, using them to promote national interests and influence public opinion abroad. In some cases, cultural diplomacy efforts may be subject to censorship or manipulation, undermining their credibility and effectiveness. Moreover, cultural diplomacy initiatives may unintentionally reinforce stereotypes or perpetuate inequalities, particularly if they fail to represent the diversity and complexity of a nation's culture. Additionally, cultural diplomacy can sometimes exacerbate cultural conflicts or tensions, especially in regions with long-standing historical grievances or identity-based divisions. Therefore, practitioners of cultural diplomacy must navigate these challenges carefully and ensure that their initiatives promote genuine dialogue, understanding, and cooperation among nations.

By harnessing the power of culture, nations can build bridges, foster mutual respect, and advance shared interests in a complex and interconnected world. However, cultural diplomacy requires careful navigation of ethical considerations, cultural sensitivities, and power dynamics to ensure its effectiveness and legitimacy as a means of promoting peace, understanding, and cooperation among nations.

Ultimately, cultural diplomacy serves as a vital tool for enhancing soft power, strengthening diplomatic ties, and shaping geopolitical landscapes in the pursuit of global stability and prosperity.

Brexit and Beyond:

Implications for European

Stability and Geopolitical Alliances

The decision of the United Kingdom to leave the European Union, known as Brexit, has reverberated across the geopolitical landscape, raising questions about the future of European stability, regional cooperation, and global alliances. In this paper, we analyse the geopolitical consequences of Brexit, exploring its impact on European unity, geopolitical alignments, and international relations beyond Europe's borders.

Brexit has strained the cohesion of the European Union, undermining the vision of an integrated and united Europe. The departure of a major member state like the UK has weakened the EU's political influence, economic clout, and strategic capabilities, diminishing its ability to shape global affairs and address common challenges. Brexit has exposed fault lines within the EU, fuelling nationalist sentiments, Euro-scepticism, and centrifugal forces that threaten to unravel the European project.

The European Union has historically served as a bulwark of stability, prosperity, and cooperation in the post-World War II era, promoting peace and reconciliation among member states through economic integration and political cooperation. However, Brexit has disrupted this unity, signalling a retreat from supranational governance and regional integration. The loss of the UK's diplomatic, economic, and military contributions weakens the EU's position on the global stage, reducing its leverage in international negotiations and weakening its ability to project power and influence beyond its borders.

Brexit has prompted geopolitical realignment in Europe, reshaping alliances, security arrangements, and power dynamics on the continent. The UK's departure from the EU has altered the balance of power within Europe, leading to shifts in diplomatic alignments and defence cooperation among EU member states. Brexit has created opportunities for other European nations, such as France and Germany, to assert leadership roles and shape the future direction of European integration and foreign policy.

Brexit has prompted a reassessment of geopolitical priorities and strategic partnerships among European nations. In the absence of the UK, traditional power brokers like France and Germany have sought to strengthen their leadership roles within the EU and assert their influence in shaping European policies and priorities. Additionally, Brexit has spurred discussions about deeper defence cooperation and security integration among EU member states, as European nations seek to enhance their collective defence capabilities and address emerging security threats, such as terrorism, cyber-attacks, and hybrid warfare.

Brexit has implications for transatlantic relations, affecting the dynamics of the EU's relationship with the United States and NATO. The UK's departure from the EU has raised questions about the future of transatlantic cooperation and the UK's role as a bridge between Europe and the United States. Brexit may lead to divergent approaches to key geopolitical issues, such as trade, climate change, and security, potentially straining relations between the EU and the US.

The UK has historically played a crucial role in facilitating transatlantic cooperation and serving as a bridge between Europe and the United States. However, Brexit introduces uncertainty into the transatlantic relationship, as the EU and the UK navigate their respective relationships with the United States and their positions on global issues. The divergence in policy priorities between the EU and the US, particularly on issues such as trade, climate change, and multilateralism, may strain transatlantic relations and complicate efforts to address shared challenges and advance common interests.

Brexit has broader implications for global governance, multilateralism, and the rules-based international order. The UK's withdrawal from the EU weakens the bloc's collective voice and influence in international institutions, diminishing its ability to promote liberal values, human rights, and multilateral cooperation on the global stage. Brexit also raises questions about the future of the rules-based international order and the effectiveness of multilateral institutions in addressing global challenges, such as climate change, migration, and pandemics.

The UK's departure from the EU diminishes the bloc's collective influence and bargaining power in international forums, such as the United Nations, the World Trade Organization, and the G7/G20 summits. As a result, the EU may struggle to advance its policy priorities and uphold its commitments to global governance, human rights, and international law. Moreover, Brexit undermines the principles of multilateralism and cooperation that underpin the rules-based international order, raising concerns about the rise of unilateralism, protectionism, and great power competition in global affairs. Therefore, Brexit represents a significant challenge to the international community's efforts to address shared challenges and uphold common values in an increasingly interconnected and interdependent world.

As Europe navigates the uncertainties and complexities of Brexit, it faces challenges and opportunities to redefine its role in the international arena, strengthen its partnerships, and uphold its commitments to peace, stability, and prosperity. By fostering dialogue, cooperation, and resilience, European nations

can navigate the geopolitical implications of
Brexit and shape a future characterized by
cooperation, solidarity, and shared prosperity in
a rapidly changing world.

United Nations or Divided States?

The Geopolitical Role of International Organizations

International organizations play a pivotal role in shaping geopolitics, facilitating cooperation, and addressing global challenges. In this paper, we examine the geopolitical significance of international organizations, focusing on the contrasting dynamics between unity and division within organizations like the United Nations (UN) and the challenges posed by competing national interests and geopolitical rivalries.

The Promise of International Organizations: International organizations, such as the United Nations, World Trade Organization, and International Monetary Fund, offer platforms for dialogue, negotiation, and cooperation among nations, aiming to promote peace, stability, and prosperity on a global scale. These organizations provide mechanisms for conflict resolution, humanitarian assistance, and development cooperation, fostering multilateralism and collective action to address transnational issues, including climate change, terrorism, and pandemics.

International organizations serve as forums for member states to address common challenges, share resources, and coordinate policies in pursuit of shared objectives. For example, the United Nations Security Council provides a platform for diplomatic negotiations and collective security measures to prevent conflicts and resolve disputes among member states. Similarly, the World Health Organization coordinates international responses to global health crises, such as the COVID-19 pandemic, by disseminating information, coordinating medical assistance, and mobilizing resources to support affected countries. By promoting cooperation and solidarity among nations, international organizations contribute to the maintenance of international peace and security and the advancement of shared interests and values.

Despite their noble objectives, international organizations often face challenges to unity and effectiveness, stemming from competing national interests, power disparities, and geopolitical rivalries among member states. Divisions within international organizations, particularly between major powers, can hinder decision-making, impede collective action, and undermine the credibility and legitimacy of these institutions.

Geopolitical rivalries and power struggles among member states can obstruct the functioning of international organizations and prevent consensus on key issues. For instance, disagreements between permanent members of the United Nations Security Council, such as the United States, Russia, and China, often lead to deadlock and inaction on critical security and humanitarian issues, such as Syria, Ukraine, and North Korea. Similarly, economic disputes and protectionist policies among member states can disrupt the functioning of organizations like the World Trade Organization, undermining efforts to promote free trade and economic cooperation. The challenge for international organizations lies in navigating these divisions and fostering consensus among member states to address global challenges and uphold the principles of multilateralism and collective security.

The United Nations occupies a central role in the geopolitics of international organizations, serving as a forum for diplomatic negotiations, conflict resolution, and peacekeeping operations. Despite its limitations and shortcomings, the UN plays a crucial role in upholding international law, promoting human rights, and providing humanitarian assistance in crisis situations around the world.

The United Nations represents the preeminent international organization tasked with maintaining peace and security, fostering development, and promoting human rights and fundamental freedoms. Through its various specialized agencies, such as the UNICEF, UNHCR, and WHO, the UN provides vital humanitarian assistance, delivers essential services, and coordinates international responses to complex emergencies, natural disasters, and conflicts. The UN Security Council, comprising five permanent members with veto powers and ten non-permanent members, holds primary responsibility for maintaining international peace and security, authorizing peacekeeping missions, and imposing sanctions on member states in cases of threats to international peace and security. Despite criticisms of its effectiveness and legitimacy, the United Nations remains indispensable in addressing global challenges and advancing collective efforts to build a more peaceful, prosperous, and sustainable world.

While these organizations offer platforms for cooperation, conflict resolution, and collective action, they also face obstacles to unity and effectiveness arising from competing national interests, power struggles, and geopolitical rivalries among member states. The role of the United Nations, in particular, remains pivotal in upholding international peace and security, promoting human rights, and addressing global challenges. By fostering dialogue, cooperation, and solidarity among nations, international organizations can overcome divisions and advance collective efforts to build a more stable, prosperous, and equitable world order.

Shifting Sands:

The Complex Geopolitical

Dynamics of the Middle East

The Middle East stands at the crossroads of history, shaped by centuries of cultural heritage, geopolitical rivalries, and strategic interests. In this paper, we delve into the intricate geopolitical dynamics of the Middle East, exploring the multifaceted interactions between states, non-state actors, and external powers that define the region's geopolitical landscape.

Historical Context: The Middle East's geopolitical dynamics are deeply rooted in its rich historical legacy, characterized by ancient civilizations, conquests, and imperial ambitions. The region's strategic location at the nexus of Europe, Asia, and Africa has made it a battleground for competing empires and civilizations throughout history, leaving behind a complex tapestry of ethnic, religious, and sectarian identities that continue to shape contemporary geopolitics.

The Middle East's geopolitical landscape is shaped by a complex interplay of historical, cultural, and geopolitical factors. The region's strategic location at the crossroads of major trade routes, such as the Silk Road and the Suez Canal, has made it a coveted prize for empires seeking to control lucrative trade routes and access to natural resources. Ancient civilizations, including Mesopotamia, Egypt, and Persia, laid the foundations for the region's cultural heritage and political identity, shaping its geopolitical dynamics and power structures over millennia.

The Middle East is marked by intense interstate rivalries and competition for power, influence, and resources among regional actors. Conflicts over territory, ideology, and hegemony have fuelled tensions and instability, leading to proxy wars, alliances, and shifting alliances that redraw the geopolitical map of the region.

The Middle East is characterized by a complex web of interstate rivalries and conflicts, driven by historical grievances, territorial disputes, and competing visions of regional order. Iran and Saudi Arabia, as two regional heavyweights, vie for influence and leadership in the Muslim world, often backing opposing factions and proxy groups in conflicts across the region, such as

Syria, Yemen, and Iraq. Similarly, the rivalry between Israel and its Arab neighbours, notably Palestine and Lebanon, shapes the geopolitics of the Levant, fuelling tensions and conflict dynamics that reverberate across the region.

The Middle East is home to a myriad of non-state actors and militant groups that challenge the authority of governments, undermine stability, and perpetuate violence and extremism. From terrorist organizations like ISIS and al-Qaeda to armed militias and insurgent groups, non-state actors exert significant influence over the region's security dynamics, complicating efforts to achieve peace and stability.

Non-state actors and militant groups play a central role in shaping the geopolitical dynamics of the Middle East, exploiting power vacuums, weak governance, and sectarian divides to advance their agendas and challenge state authority. Groups like ISIS (Islamic State of Iraq and Syria) and al-Qaeda have exploited regional conflicts, sectarian tensions, and social grievances to establish footholds and recruit followers, posing threats to regional stability and international security. Armed militias and insurgent groups, backed by external sponsors and patrons, further complicate efforts to resolve conflicts and establish stable governance structures, perpetuating cycles of violence and instability.

The Middle East is a battleground for competing external powers seeking to advance their strategic interests, influence regional outcomes, and shape the balance of power. Great power rivalries, geopolitical competitions, and interventions exacerbate tensions, fuel conflicts, and complicate efforts to achieve peace and stability in the region.

External interventions by global powers, including the United States, Russia, China, and European nations, have profound implications for the geopolitical dynamics of the Middle East. Great power rivalries, geopolitical competitions, and interventions exacerbate existing tensions, fuel conflicts, and perpetuate instability in the region. For example, the US and Russia compete for influence in Syria, backing opposing factions and conducting military operations that exacerbate the humanitarian crisis and prolong the conflict. Similarly, China's economic investments and infrastructure projects in the region, through initiatives like the Belt and Road Initiative, reflect its growing geopolitical ambitions and strategic interests in securing access to energy resources and expanding its influence along key trade routes.

The Complex Geopolitical Dynamics of the Middle East highlights the intricate interplay of historical legacies, interstate rivalries, non-state actors, and external interventions that define the region's geopolitical landscape. As the Middle East grapples with on-going conflicts, political transitions, and social transformations, understanding the complexities of its geopolitical dynamics is essential for formulating effective strategies to promote peace, stability, and prosperity in the region. By fostering dialogue, cooperation, and inclusive governance, regional and international actors can mitigate tensions, address root causes of conflict, and build a more secure and resilient Middle East for future generations.

A Continent in Transition:

Africa's Emerging Geopolitical Landscape

Africa's geopolitical landscape in the 21st century is marked by a profound transformation, characterized by shifting power dynamics, economic growth, and geopolitical competition. In this paper, we explore the emerging geopolitical trends shaping Africa's trajectory, examining the continent's evolving role in global affairs and the opportunities and challenges it faces in navigating a rapidly changing world order.

Africa's geopolitical landscape is deeply influenced by its colonial past, post-independence struggles, and diverse cultural, linguistic, and ethnic identities. The legacy of colonialism, which carved up the continent into artificial boundaries and exploited its resources, continues to shape contemporary geopolitical dynamics, fuelling conflicts, border disputes, and governance challenges.

Africa's colonial history has left a lasting impact on its geopolitical landscape, shaping its political boundaries, economic structures, and social fabric. Colonial powers, including Britain, France, Portugal, and Belgium, imposed arbitrary borders and divided ethnic groups, tribes, and communities, leading to unresolved territorial disputes, ethnic tensions, and governance challenges that persist to this day. The struggle for independence and decolonization movements in the mid-20th century laid the groundwork for Africa's nation-building efforts and efforts to assert sovereignty and self-determination, but also left behind a legacy of political instability, corruption, and underdevelopment that continues to shape the continent's geopolitical realities.

Africa's geopolitical landscape is being reshaped by the rise of regional powers and economic blocs seeking to assert influence, promote integration, and address common challenges. Countries like Nigeria, South Africa, Kenya, and Ethiopia are emerging as regional powerhouses, driving economic growth, political stability, and regional cooperation within their respective spheres of influence.

The rise of regional powers in Africa reflects the continent's growing assertiveness and ambition to play a greater role in shaping its own destiny. Countries like Nigeria, as the largest economy in West Africa, and South Africa, as the most industrialized economy in Southern Africa, wield significant influence within their respective regions and serve as anchors for regional integration and cooperation initiatives, such as the Economic Community of West African States (ECOWAS) and the Southern African Development Community (SADC). Similarly, Ethiopia's strategic location and economic dynamism position it as a key player in East Africa, driving infrastructure development, trade facilitation, and diplomatic engagement with neighbouring countries. As these regional powers assert their influence and pursue common objectives, they are reshaping Africa's geopolitical landscape and challenging traditional power dynamics within the continent.

Africa's geopolitical landscape is characterized by intense competition among external powers seeking to advance their strategic interests, access to resources, and influence in the region. China, Russia, the United States, and European nations are actively engaged in Africa, pursuing diplomatic, economic, and military partnerships that shape the continent's development trajectory and geopolitical alignments.

Africa's strategic importance, abundant natural resources, and growing markets have made it a focal point of geopolitical competition and rivalry among global powers. China's Belt and Road Initiative (BRI), for example, has led to extensive investments in infrastructure, energy, and telecommunications projects across Africa, enhancing China's economic footprint and influence on the continent. Similarly, Russia has sought to strengthen its military presence and strategic partnerships in Africa, leveraging arms sales, energy cooperation, and diplomatic ties to expand its influence and counter Western influence in the region. The United States and European nations, meanwhile, continue to maintain economic ties, security partnerships, and development assistance programs in Africa, albeit facing competition from emerging powers and increased scrutiny over their engagement strategies. As external powers vie for influence and access in Africa, they shape the continent's geopolitical alignments, economic development, and security dynamics, influencing its trajectory in the 21st century.

Challenges and Opportunities: Africa's geopolitical landscape presents both challenges and opportunities for the continent's development and stability. Persistent conflicts, governance challenges, and socioeconomic disparities threaten to undermine Africa's potential, while regional integration, economic diversification, and diplomatic engagement offer pathways to prosperity, peace, and resilience.

Africa faces a myriad of challenges, including conflicts, political instability, corruption, poverty, and environmental degradation, which hinder its development and undermine its geopolitical influence. Weak governance structures, inadequate infrastructure, and limited access to education and healthcare exacerbate these challenges, perpetuating cycles of poverty and underdevelopment in many parts of the continent. However, Africa also possesses vast opportunities for growth and transformation, including its youthful population, natural resources, and untapped market potential. Regional integration efforts, such as the African Continental Free Trade Area (AfCFTA), hold promise for fostering economic integration, trade facilitation, and investment promotion across the continent, unlocking new opportunities for shared prosperity and sustainable development. Diplomatic engagement with external partners, such as China, India, and the Gulf states, offers avenues for infrastructure financing, technology transfer, and capacity-building that can support Africa's development objectives and enhance its geopolitical relevance in global affairs.

"A Continent in Transition: Africa's Emerging Geopolitical Landscape" underscores the complexities and opportunities inherent in Africa's evolving geopolitical dynamics. As the continent navigates the challenges of the 21st century, including conflicts, governance deficits, and socioeconomic disparities, it also stands at a critical juncture for realizing its potential and shaping its own destiny. By fostering regional cooperation, economic diversification, and inclusive development, Africa can harness its resources, talents, and partnerships to build a more prosperous, peaceful, and resilient continent that contributes to global stability and prosperity. As Africa emerges as a key player in global affairs, its geopolitical choices and actions will have far-reaching implications for the continent and the world at large.

In the Shadow of Giants:

Latin America's Geopolitical

Position between the US and China

Latin America finds itself at a crucial juncture in the 21st century, caught between the competing influences of two global superpowers, the United States and China. In this paper, we delve into the complex geopolitical dynamics of Latin America, examining the region's strategic importance, economic ties, and diplomatic relations with the US and China.

Latin America's geopolitical landscape has been shaped by centuries of colonialism, independence movements, and Cold War rivalries. The Monroe Doctrine, articulated by the United States in the 19th century, asserted its hegemony over the Western Hemisphere, while the Cuban Revolution and the rise of leftist movements in the 20th century challenged US dominance and led to geopolitical tensions in the region.

Latin America's historical relationship with the United States has been characterized by a mix of cooperation, intervention, and resistance. The Monroe Doctrine, proclaimed in 1823, asserted US hegemony over the Western Hemisphere and warned European powers against interference in the affairs of independent Latin American nations. Throughout the 20th century, the US wielded its economic and military power to influence political developments in Latin America, supporting friendly governments, suppressing leftist movements, and intervening militarily in countries like Guatemala, Chile, and Nicaragua. However, the rise of populist leaders and leftist governments in the region, such as Hugo Chávez in Venezuela and Evo Morales in Bolivia, challenged US hegemony and fostered anti-American sentiment, leading to strained relations and ideological divisions in the region.

China's emergence as a global economic powerhouse has reshaped Latin America's geopolitical landscape, offering new opportunities for trade, investment, and development cooperation. Chinese investments in infrastructure, energy, and natural resources have fuelled economic growth in Latin America, but also raised concerns about debt dependency, environmental sustainability, and political influence.

China's growing presence in Latin America reflects its strategic interests in securing access to natural resources, expanding its market reach, and countering US influence in the region. China's Belt and Road Initiative (BRI), a global infrastructure and investment program, has led to significant investments in Latin American countries, particularly in sectors like energy, transportation, and telecommunications. Chinese loans, grants, and investments have financed major infrastructure projects, such as ports, railways, and hydroelectric dams, providing much-needed capital and technology to support Latin America's development aspirations. However, China's economic engagement in the region has also raised concerns about debt sustainability, environmental degradation, and social impacts, prompting calls for greater transparency, accountability, and responsible investment practices.

Latin American countries navigate a delicate diplomatic balancing act between the United

States and China, seeking to maximize economic opportunities, maintain political autonomy, and safe-guard national sovereignty. Many countries in the region pursue a diversified foreign policy, engaging with multiple partners and regional blocs to mitigate dependence on any single power.

Latin American countries adopt nuanced approaches to managing their relationships with the United States and China, recognizing the benefits of economic cooperation while safeguarding their political autonomy and sovereignty. Some countries, like Brazil and Mexico, prioritize economic ties with China as a means of diversifying their trade partners and attracting foreign investment, while maintaining strategic partnerships with the United States on security and defence issues. Others, such as Chile and Peru, leverage their natural resource wealth to attract Chinese investments in mining and energy projects, while cultivating diplomatic relations with the US to promote democratic governance and human rights. Regional blocs like the Community of Latin American and Caribbean States (CELAC) and the Pacific Alliance serve as forums for promoting regional integration, economic cooperation, and dialogue among Latin American nations, providing opportunities for collective engagement with external powers and safeguarding regional interests.

"In the Shadow of Giants: Latin America's Geopolitical Position Between the US and China" highlights the complexities and opportunities inherent in Latin America's geopolitical dynamics. As the region navigates the competing influences of the United States and China, it faces challenges and opportunities to advance its economic development, political autonomy, and regional integration. By adopting a pragmatic and balanced approach to diplomacy, Latin American countries can harness the benefits of engagement with both superpowers while safeguarding their sovereignty and promoting regional interests. As Latin America emerges as a key player in global affairs, its geopolitical choices and actions will shape the future trajectory of the region and its relations with the rest of the world.

Cold Front:

The Rising Geopolitical Importance

of the Arctic Region

The Arctic region is undergoing profound changes driven by climate change, melting ice, and resource exploration, leading to increased geopolitical competition and strategic interest among Arctic and non-Arctic states. In this paper, we examine the emerging geopolitical importance of the Arctic, exploring the strategic implications of changing environmental conditions and shifting power dynamics in the region.

Climate change is transforming the Arctic landscape, leading to melting ice caps, retreating glaciers, and opening up new maritime routes and resource extraction opportunities. These changes are reshaping the geopolitical dynamics of the Arctic, as states seek to exploit economic opportunities, assert territorial claims, and address environmental challenges.

The Arctic is warming at a faster rate than the global average, leading to the rapid melting of sea ice and the opening up of previously inaccessible areas for shipping, fishing, and resource extraction. The retreat of Arctic ice caps has fuelled competition among Arctic and non-Arctic states for control over valuable resources, including oil, gas, minerals, and fish stocks. As the Arctic becomes more accessible, states are vying for territorial claims and exclusive economic zones (EEZs) in the region, leading to disputes over maritime boundaries and sovereignty rights. Moreover, the melting ice has raised concerns about environmental degradation, habitat loss, and the impact of climate change on indigenous communities and ecosystems in the Arctic.

The Arctic's abundant natural resources, including oil, gas, minerals, and fish, have attracted the attention of states and corporations seeking to exploit economic opportunities in the region. The potential for resource extraction in the Arctic has sparked competition among Arctic states and raised questions about environmental sustainability, indigenous rights, and responsible governance.

The Arctic is estimated to hold significant reserves of oil, gas, minerals, and other valuable resources, making it an attractive destination for energy companies, mining firms, and commercial fishing fleets. Arctic states, including Russia, Canada, Norway, Denmark, and the United States, have initiated exploration and development projects in the region to capitalize on these resources and stimulate economic growth. However, the pursuit of resource extraction in the Arctic poses environmental risks, including the threat of oil spills, habitat destruction, and pollution, which could have far-reaching consequences for the fragile Arctic ecosystem and indigenous communities dependent on traditional livelihoods. Moreover, competition for resource access has heightened tensions among Arctic states and raised concerns about territorial disputes, military build-ups, and geopolitical rivalries in the region.

The changing geopolitical dynamics of the Arctic have led to increased military activity and strategic competition among Arctic and non-Arctic states. The Arctic's strategic location and potential for resource extraction have raised concerns about security risks, military build-ups, and the militarization of the region.

The Arctic's strategic significance as a potential transit route for shipping and resource extraction has prompted Arctic and non-Arctic states to enhance their military presence and surveillance capabilities in the region. Russia, in particular, has invested heavily in modernizing its Arctic infrastructure, deploying troops, and conducting military exercises to assert its sovereignty and protect its strategic interests in the region. NATO members, including the United States, Canada, and Norway, have also bolstered their military presence in the Arctic, conducting joint patrols, exercises, and surveillance missions to safeguard their security interests and deter potential threats. The militarization of the Arctic has raised concerns about the risk of conflict escalation, arms races, and the potential for accidents or incidents that could undermine regional stability and cooperation.

The Arctic's emerging geopolitical importance has highlighted the need for effective governance mechanisms and international cooperation to address common challenges,

protect the environment, and promote
sustainable development in the region. However,
governance gaps, competing interests, and
geopolitical tensions pose obstacles to achieving
consensus and cooperation among Arctic states
and stakeholders.

The Arctic is governed by a complex web of
international agreements, treaties, and
organizations, including the Arctic Council, which
coordinates cooperation among Arctic states on
environmental protection, scientific research,
and sustainable development in the region.
However, governance challenges, including
overlapping jurisdictional claims, competing
interests, and geopolitical tensions, hinder
efforts to address common challenges and
promote multilateral cooperation in the Arctic.
Disputes over territorial claims, resource
extraction, and shipping routes have strained
relations among Arctic states, leading to
diplomatic tensions and rivalries that complicate
efforts to achieve consensus on key issues.
Moreover, the involvement of non-Arctic states,
such as China and Russia, in Arctic affairs adds
another layer of complexity to governance
dynamics, raising questions about transparency,

accountability, and respect for Arctic sovereignty and indigenous rights.

The Rising Geopolitical Importance of the Arctic Region" underscores the complex interplay of environmental, economic, and security factors shaping the Arctic's geopolitical landscape. As the Arctic undergoes rapid changes driven by climate change and resource exploration, states and stakeholders must navigate competing interests, address governance challenges, and promote international cooperation to ensure sustainable development and environmental protection in the region. By fostering dialogue, transparency, and respect for Arctic sovereignty and indigenous rights, the international community can work together to mitigate risks, promote peace, and preserve the unique ecosystem of the Arctic for future generations.

Storytelling States:

The Role of Geopolitical Narratives

in Shaping National Identity

Geopolitical narratives play a crucial role in shaping national identity, influencing perceptions of history, culture, and geopolitical positioning. In this paper, we explore how states use storytelling and narrative construction to define their national identity, assert their geopolitical interests, and shape public discourse on domestic and international affairs.

States often construct narratives of historical legitimacy to justify their territorial claims, political systems, and national identity. These narratives draw on historical events, myths, and symbols to create a sense of continuity, collective memory, and identity among citizens.

Geopolitical narratives of historical legitimacy serve to reinforce the legitimacy and authority of the state, legitimizing its territorial boundaries, political institutions, and cultural heritage. For example, countries like China and Russia emphasize historical narratives of empire, conquest, and civilization to assert their claims to territorial sovereignty and regional hegemony. Similarly, nations like the United States and France construct narratives of democratic values, freedom, and human rights to justify their geopolitical interventions and promote their national identity as champions of liberty and democracy. These narratives not only shape domestic perceptions of national identity but also influence international relations and geopolitical alliances, as states seek to project a positive image of themselves and garner support for their geopolitical objectives.

Geopolitical narratives often incorporate elements of identity politics and cultural narratives to reinforce national unity, cohesion, and solidarity. States use cultural symbols, traditions, and historical figures to create a shared sense of belonging and collective identity among diverse populations.

Cultural narratives and identity politics play a central role in shaping national identity and geopolitical narratives, as states seek to foster a sense of unity and belonging among citizens from diverse ethnic, linguistic, and religious backgrounds. For example, countries like India and Brazil highlight cultural diversity and multiculturalism in their geopolitical narratives, celebrating cultural festivals, traditions, and heritage sites as symbols of national unity and strength. Similarly, nations like Japan and South Korea draw on historical narratives of resilience, sacrifice, and national pride to promote a sense of solidarity and identity among citizens in the face of external threats and geopolitical challenges. By emphasizing cultural narratives and identity politics, states seek to strengthen social cohesion, foster national pride, and bolster support for their geopolitical agendas.

Geopolitical narratives play a crucial role in shaping international perceptions of states and influencing diplomatic relations, alliances, and conflicts. States use narrative diplomacy to promote their geopolitical interests, counter negative stereotypes, and build soft power and influence on the world stage.

Geopolitical narratives serve as a tool of statecraft in international relations, as states seek to shape global perceptions of their identity, values, and geopolitical objectives. For example, countries like China and Russia engage in narrative diplomacy to promote alternative narratives of global governance, sovereignty, and development that challenge Western hegemony and promote their own geopolitical interests. Similarly, nations like the United States and European countries use narrative diplomacy to project a positive image of themselves as defenders of democracy, human rights, and international law, seeking to garner support for their geopolitical objectives and build alliances with like-minded states. Geopolitical narratives also play a role in shaping public opinion, media coverage, and international discourse on key issues, influencing public perceptions of states and shaping diplomatic negotiations and policy decisions.

"Storytelling States: The Role of Geopolitical Narratives in Shaping National Identity" highlights the importance of narrative construction and storytelling in shaping national identity, influencing public perceptions, and shaping international relations. By understanding the power of geopolitical narratives, states can leverage narrative diplomacy to promote their geopolitical interests, build soft power, and shape public discourse on domestic and international affairs. However, the manipulation of narratives for political purposes also poses risks, as it can lead to the spread of misinformation, polarization, and conflict escalation in international relations. Therefore, it is essential for states to engage in responsible narrative construction that promotes dialogue, understanding, and cooperation among nations, fostering a more peaceful and interconnected world order.